Unlock the Success Code to Influence Principles

*Practical and Proven Examples to
Ethically Persuade in Business and Life*

Helping Entrepreneurs and Authors Easily Publish Their Book

"This inspiring book reveals how giving and ethical influence can transform your relationships, career, and life. Apply its lessons to lead with purpose and create lasting success." — **BRIAN TRACY, Author, Speaker, Consultant**

Unlock the Success Code to Influence Principles

Practical and Proven Examples to Ethically Persuade in Business and Life

Foreword by Roger Dooley, Author of *Friction and Brainfluence*

Sprague | Fabon | Maier | Bushin | Younggren | Sidell

© Copyright 2025

By Duane "DJ" Sprague, Al Fabon, Maria Maier, Vladimir Bushin, Christian Younggren, Ellin Sidell

Edited by James North

All rights reserved.

Book Layout ©2025

Published by: Evolve Global Publishing

www.EvolveGlobalPublishing.com

No part of this book may be reproduced or transmitted in any form or by any means, electronic or mechanical, including photocopying, recording or by any information storage and retrieval system, without written permission from the authors, except for the inclusion of brief quotations in a review.

Limit of Liability Disclaimer: The information contained in this book is for information purposes only, and may not apply to your situation. The author, publisher, distributor, and provider provide no warranty about the content or accuracy of the content enclosed. The information provided is subjective. Keep this in mind when reviewing this guide. Neither the Publisher nor the Author shall be liable for any loss of profit or any other commercial damages resulting from the use of this guide. All links are for information purposes only and are not warranted for content, accuracy, or any other implied or explicit purpose.

Earnings Disclaimer: All income examples in this book are examples. They are not intended to represent or guarantee that everyone will achieve the same results. You understand that each individual's success will be determined by his or her desire, dedication, background, effort, and motivation to work. There is no guarantee you will duplicate any of the results stated here. You recognize any business endeavours have inherent risk or loss of capital.

No part of this book may be used or reproduced in any manner for the purpose of training artificial intelligence technologies or systems. In accordance with Article 4(3) of the Digital Single Market Directive 2019/790, Evolve Global Publishing expressly reserves this work from the text and data mining exception.

The Influence Advantage

Unlock the Success Code to Influence Principles

Practical and Proven Examples to Ethically Persuade in Business and Life

1st Edition. 2025 v2.4

ASIN: B0DTJ1Y6BY (Amazon Kindle)

ISBN: 978-1-923223-48-6 (eBook)

ISBN: 978-1-923223-49-3 (Amazon Paperback)

ISBN: 978-1-923223-50-9 (Amazon Hardcover)

ISBN: 978-1-923223-51-6 (Ingram Spark) PAPERBACK

ISBN: 978-1-923223-52-3 (Ingram Spark) HARDCOVER

TRADEMARKS

All product names, logos, and brands are the property of their respective owners. All company, product, and service names used in this book are for identification purposes only. Using these names, logos, and brands does not imply endorsement. All other trademarks cited herein are the property of their respective owners.

Table of Contents

About the Authors 7

Endorsements for The Influence Advantage 9

Acknowledgements 15

Foreword 19

About the Author: Duane "DJ" Sprague 23

Ecommerce Success Starts Here 25

About the Author: Al Fabon 41

Give More First 43

About the Author: Maria Maier 57

From Adversity to Abundance 59

About the Author: Vladimir Bushin 71

Liking is King 73

About the Author: Christian Younggren 87

The Experience Trap: When Too Much Sales
Knowledge Becomes a Blindspot 89

About the Author: Ellin Sidell 101

3 Winning Influence Strategies in Fortune 500 Companies 103

Epilogue 115

Glossary 119

Index 123

About the Authors

Duane "DJ" Sprague

Vladimir Bushin

Al Fabon

Christian Younggren

Maria Maier

Ellin Sidell

Endorsements for The Influence Advantage

In my 30-plus years of working with leaders and entrepreneurs around the world, I've seen firsthand the profound impact that ethical influence can have on both personal and professional success.

The Influence Advantage brilliantly demonstrates this truth. The authors, each with a wealth of experience and expertise in their fields, share not only powerful strategies for leadership and business growth but also a deep commitment to serving others with integrity and purpose. I've always said, "Who you learn from matters."

This book combines the science of human behavior with the author's real-world, actionable insights, making it an invaluable resource for anyone seeking to understand and apply the principles of influence.

What truly stands out, however, is the genuine passion these authors have for helping others succeed. Whether it's through building trust, fostering unity, or offering guidance in times of adversity, the lessons within these pages are all grounded in a desire to make a positive, lasting impact on the lives of others.

I've had the honor and privilege of having a front-row seat to their journey of personal and professional growth and have seen how the power of ethical influence has opened doors for each of them.

If you're looking for a guide to lead with integrity, build stronger relationships, and create meaningful influence in your work and life, this book is for you. I'm confident it will not only inspire you but also equip you with the tools you need to achieve your fullest potential while serving those around you.

- **Paul Martinelli, Internationally Acclaimed Speaker, Trainer, Mentor, and Coach, Founder of the Empowered Living Community, World's # 1 Business Coach - Global Gurus**

This inspiring book reveals how giving and ethical influence can transform your relationships, career, and life. Apply its lessons to lead with purpose and create lasting success.

- **Brian Tracy, Author / Speaker / Consultant**

The Influence Advantage masterfully transforms complex influence principles into clear, immediately applicable strategies. By combining behavioral science with compelling real-world applications, each chapter provides a unique roadmap for creating authentic impact across any industry. This refreshing approach makes sophisticated influence techniques accessible and actionable for everyone, from emerging leaders to seasoned executives.

- **Dr. Justin James Kennedy, Professor, Behavioural Neuroscience, Master Neuroplastician®**

A powerful guide to building authentic connections, fostering collaboration, and transforming adversity into growth. With 30 years of experience as a leader and coach for a Fortune 100 company, I can confidently say this book is essential reading for anyone seeking meaningful personal and professional transformation.

- **Brad Dufrane, ChFC CLU CLF FSCP LUTCF, Managing Partner, New York Life Insurance Company, Author**

This book makes complex concepts accessible and immediately actionable by translating Cialdini's principles into impactful strategies. It's an invaluable guide for anyone looking to leverage ethical influence for business success.

- Lee Roquest, CEO of Finch.com--Ecommerce Growth Experts

The Influence Advantage is a unique read. While many books on leadership topics are theoretical, with occasional stories woven in, this book is completely to the opposite. The various authors teach well and base their teachings on life experiences that the reader can resonate with. As you read this book, try to put yourselves into their stories. Try to understand why they reacted the way they did and how you can use their experiences and successes to apply to situations in your professional and personal path.

- Karl Pister, PCC, Founder and President, The Coaching Group, Inc.

The Influence Advantage is packed with real-life, actionable insights and dives into ethical influence with tools you can actually use—straightforward, real, and powerful. A must-read if you're ready to improve your impact in business and life. It's truly a masterclass in using trust to drive growth in today's complex business world.

- Lauren Petrullo, MBA, Owner of Mongoose Media, Co-Host of Perpetual Traffic Podcast, and Global Speaker

The Influence Advantage is packed with real, usable advice for anyone looking to make a genuine impact. Each chapter combines science-backed strategies with everyday examples that show how influence works in practical terms, whether you're in business or just want to connect better with others. It's quite refreshing to see a book that prioritizes ethics in influence - definitely worth the read for anyone who wants to lead authentically and effectively.

- Barbara Gustavson, Corporate Wellness Trainer

By weaving together behavioral science insights and real-world examples, The Influence Advantage delivers powerful, actionable strategies that apply across every industry. Each chapter explores distinct principles of influence that will inspire and equip you to build trust, drive engagement, and achieve lasting success. This book is a must-read for anyone looking to elevate their leadership and impact through ethical influence! Grab your copy today and transform the way you influence and lead!

- Brian Bartes, Success Coach, Bestselling Author, and Host of the Podcast, "LifeExcellence with Brian Bartes"

Six Cialdini Certified Coaches and Practitioners sharing their insights on influence and persuasion in one place? Run, don't walk, to get your copy of The Influence Advantage.

- Melina Palmer, CEO of The Brainy Business and author of What Your Customer Wants and Can't Tell You

Having delivered training to over 15,000 small business owners worldwide who work with corporate clients, I know that one essential element of success is the ability to influence. The Influence Advantage is an invaluable guide for mastering this skill, especially in today's world that is transforming overnight. The authors bring Cialdini's principles to life with compelling examples, showing how behavioral science can be applied with integrity to drive real change. From navigating high-stakes meetings to building trust with clients, this book empowers leaders, business owners, innovators and thought leaders at every level to ethically expand their impact. It's an essential tool for those who want to lead and succeed in any industry — and a transformative addition to the conversation on ethical influence.

- Angelique Rewers, CEO, BoldHaus

The Influence Advantage is a transformative guide that resonates deeply with leaders across diverse fields. Drawing from my decades of leadership experience in both senior roles within Fortune 100 companies and as a clinician in emergency medicine, I found this book to be a masterclass in practical, actionable wisdom. It contains invaluable strategies for cultivating "ethical" influence and also emphasizes the power of persistence and grit. This book is a must-read.

- Rich Arriaga MS, BS-Bio., BSN, RN

Our world keeps getting more noisy and more crowded, especially in the online business space. The Influence Advantage is the secret key to unlocking new levels of growth through the proven power of ethical influence and persuasion.

- Dustin Riechmann, Founder of 7-Figure Leap

Regardless of your experience in business or leadership, the ability to influence others is critical to reaching lasting agreements. The Influence Advantage is a powerful collaboration of diverse perspectives. As a negotiation coach, author, and former military commander, I've learned to embrace the personal experiences of dedicated professionals. If you have a growth mindset and a desire to improve, this is a must-read.

- Jim Camp Jr., Owner Camp Negotiations, Author of "Lead from No", Major General USAF (retired)

Without trust, we don't believe—and without belief, we're closed off to ethical influence and persuasion. In this insightful and practical collection, The Influence Advantage offers real-world examples grounded in behavioral science. A must-read for leaders seeking actionable wisdom.

- Natalie Doyle Oldfield, Best Selling Author, Trusted The Proven Path to Customer Loyalty and Business Growth

This is not just another book on persuasion psychology; it's a compilation of real-world examples and outcomes from business people who applied simple techniques in various situations and industries to get a 'yes.' If you want to improve your outcomes and relationships, regardless of your business or industry, this is the book to read.

- Matthew Stafford, CEO of BuildGrowScale.com

Acknowledgements

We are deeply grateful for the pioneers, teachers, mentors, and authors of behavioral science who have illuminated the path forward for the day-to-day practitioners of consumer psychology, decision-making, and ethical persuasion.

These icons and their contributions to the field of consumer psychology have deeply enriched this exciting field of knowledge, research, and case studies, and we wish to acknowledge their contributions to the field and their inspiration for our collective experiences and work brought forth in this book.

Dr. Robert Cialdini for his seminal work and publication of the NYT Best Selling 'Influence' and 'Pre-Suasion' and the Cialdini Institute's training programs.

Roger Dooley for his foreword, his training videos on the CXL Institute, and his books 'Friction' and 'Brainfluence.'

Bas Wouters and Joris Groen for their groundbreaking publication of 'Online Influence' and the Online Influence Institute.

Our appreciation and acknowledgment to Dr. Chris Phelps, the US CEO of Cialdini Institute, for the continuous support of the book idea and ongoing questions. We appreciate the collaboration and encouragement.

Rory Sutherland for his applications, insights, and examples from observations and applications of the principles as an "Ad Man," his classic book 'Alchemy,' and his videos on the Mindworx Academy.

Jim Camp Jr. for his visionary leadership book "Lead From NO, a Systematic Approach to Leadership Negotiation" and his remarkable contrarian coaching.

We also would like to recognize the influence of Dr. BJ Fogg, Dr. Daniel Kahneman, and Dr. Dan Ariely for their research, literary works, and vast contributions to the understanding of human persuasion and decision-making.

Dr. John C. Maxwell for featuring Dr. Robert B. Cialdini at the International Maxwell Certification stage. Being in the room with the world's foremost leadership and influence experts is an affirmation that leadership and influence are intertwined.

As certified coaches and practitioners from the Cialdini Institute, among a variety of other behavioral science institutions, we are deeply grateful for the impact these principles of ethical influence have had on our personal and professional lives.

We are also grateful for the support from our families, who have given us the latitude to bring this work forward and continue sharing the power of these timeless principles.

I am so thankful for my husband, David, and my daughters, Kelsey and Marissa for supporting me (Ellin Sidell) and helping me make my dreams come true.

First and foremost, my (Maria Maier's) deepest gratitude goes to my incredible family. To my husband, Jeff - your unwavering support and belief in me have been my anchor through every step of this journey. To my mother, Larisa - thank you for your endless encouragement and love, which have always been a source of strength. And to my children - Victoria, Peter, Robert, and Katrina - you are my greatest inspiration. You remind me daily to strive for more, to give my best, and to leave a meaningful impact on the world. To my mentor, Paul Martinelli - your wisdom, guidance, and belief in my potential have profoundly shaped not only the creation of this book but also my journey as an entrepreneur. Dr. Rick Ruperto, for championing my dreams with such generosity and faith.

A huge and heartfelt thank you to my (Al Fabon's) mother for her unwavering support and endless love and to my brother and sisters for being my biggest cheerleaders.

A warm, loving thank you to my (Vladimir Bushin's) father and mother for wisdom and kindness, leading me to this moment.

And finally, we are grateful for you, the reader - thank you for allowing us to share The Influence Advantage journey with you. We hope this book adds value to your business and your life.

Foreword

By Roger Dooley, author of Friction and Brainfluence

A few years before a young professor named Robert Cialdini went undercover to learn the techniques employed by used car dealers, fundraisers, and other real-world persuasion experts, I was a callow college student studying engineering and minoring in psychology. The single class I remember from my minor's coursework was one called "The Psychology of Persuasion." I was intrigued by advertising and its ability to change consumer behavior and wanted to understand how it worked. For one project in that class, I created ads for a Pittsburgh florist designed to appeal to customer emotions. They are lost to time, but I'm fairly sure the fictional Don Draper of Mad Men wouldn't have hired me.

At that time, there was no textbook that focused on persuasion psychology. We studied research papers on persuasion and drew on books like those by Dale Carnegie and Vance Packard. Cialdini's seminal book Influence finally filled the need for a definitive text in the persuasion space. Based on a combination of academic research and what Cialdini learned from real-world persuaders, the book has since sold millions of copies. Influence became the foundation of most of the thinking on ethical persuasion.

The book you are about to read, The Influence Advantage, takes Cialdini's work to a new level. It explains, in detail, how to apply the principles of ethical persuasion to your business and personal life. This book is a compilation of insights and case studies by individual Certified Coaches and Practitioners of the Cialdini Institute, who have used these principles to achieve remarkable results.

No one fits this description better than my friend and colleague, DJ Sprague. His wide-ranging first chapter describes the concept of pre-suasion, introduced by Cialdini decades after Influence was first released. Sprague shows how this concept and Cialdini's principles can be applied to the rapidly changing world of e-commerce, search engine optimization, reputation management, and other aspects of digital marketing.

Friction, unnecessary effort in any process, is often overlooked by marketers, but not Sprague. He dubs it "The Silent Killer" and makes the important connection to trust. Lower levels of trust result in more friction. Sprague describes its pernicious effects on converting browsers into buyers and explains how to create a frictionless online shopping experience to maximize revenue.

Other notable authors, Certified Coaches, and Practitioners of the Cialdini principles add their own powerful insights and personal experiences of applying these timeless consumer psychology principles to the Influence Advantage.

Al Fabon delves deep into the reciprocity principle with several personal examples of how he advanced his career and life and became more productive as a college instructor and later a manager and consultant by leveraging reciprocity and gift-giving. He implements these principles, however, in very unusual and unexpected ways that cost nothing while paying huge dividends.

Maria Maier draws on her diverse career in both Russia and the USA to reveal how ethical influence has been key to transforming setbacks into opportunities. As an executive coach and growth consultant she passionately equips international business leaders with actionable strategies to harness resilience and ethical influence for lasting success in today's competitive global market.

Vladimir Bushin, an expert negotiator, shares his experience of how the principle of liking equates to money and how it makes the difference between winning or losing contracts, being promoted or losing the job, and getting invited or being forgotten. He also shows how liking relates to respect and how to build a path from negative relationships into positive ones.

Christian Younggren, a professional sales trainer, demonstrates how subconscious cognitive biases can cloud our judgment and curtail a lucrative sales career when left unchecked. He exposes how system 1 thinking, representativeness bias, confirmation bias, social proof, and the say-do dilemma can creep into our sales process and decision-making, only to cap our income-earning potential.

Ellin Sidell, CEO of The Sidell Method, shares her inspiring stories of how she used the influence principles of authority, social proof, liking, and contrast to get more "yeses" while contributing to the growth of multi-billion brands and advancing her career at Nestle, Microsoft, and Costco. And how she uses these principles to guide her clients to more tremendous success.

The concepts in this book apply to organizations of any size, from startups to global enterprises. Humans populate all companies, and the levers that change behavior and lead to action are universal across cultures, nations, and demographics.

This book will show you how to use the principles of persuasion to achieve your goals and positively impact the world. I highly recommend it to anyone who wants an up-to-the-minute, entirely practical guide to ideas that have stood the test of time.

About the Author: Duane "DJ" Sprague

Duane "DJ" Sprague has over 35 years of experience in online and offline marketing, advertising, sales, and PR on the client and agency side with Kodak, Toyota, Hyundai, and JD Power, as well as sports franchises, including the NBA, MLS, and NASCAR.

DJ is a keynote speaker, podcaster, and co-author of Reputation King, several academic marketing books, author of industry ebooks, and CMO of Shopper Approved.

He helps website executives compound their growth by implementing proven online reputation management, integrated marketing, and behavioral science principles that improve paid and organic search results, traffic, conversions, and revenue, including a 7.5x revenue growth in 4 years, from $7M to $54M.

DJ holds an MS degree in Integrated Marketing Communications and has also earned over 70 professional certifications and mini degrees, including Certified Ecommerce Marketing Expert, and Digital Psychology & Persuasion by the CXL Institute, Ethical Influence Coach and Professional by the Cialdini Institute, Online Influence and Behavioral Design Coach and Practitioner by the Online Influence Institute, plus certifications in consumer psychology from the Behavioral Design Academy, the Mindworx Academy, and many more.

Chapter 1

Ecommerce Success Starts Here

by Duane "DJ" Sprague

Your Online Success—Or Failure—Starts Here

The buyer's journey, or conversion path, often begins in the search results. Here, the buyer will decide which results to click based on various subconscious trust-emitting factors.

This is the moment of truth...Because an online business is statistically bound to fail without properly and proactively addressing this critical first step of the conversion path.

Here's why.

The first step of the conversion path is how and where you appear in the search results, and if you don't get this right, you lose.

The first organic listing, for example, gets 11.5x more traffic than the tenth position (Backlinko), while organic listings with review stars see an increase in click-through rate of 13-35% (CXL Institute), and paid ads with review stars get 10-35% more clicks (Google). And that's just the beginning.

In summary, star ratings in the search results can help businesses earn trust from potential customers, improve local search rankings, and boost conversions (Search Engine Journal).

A Cautionary Tale

Despite the many celebrated ecommerce successes, the truth is that online businesses fail at an astonishing rate:

- 90% of ecommerce website start-ups fail in less than four months (Entrepreneur Magazine).
- 90% of A/B split tests not based on behavioral science principles fail to produce positive conversion results (Online Influence Institute).

However, if you simply embrace the psychology of influence, neither of these high failure rate statistics has to be true.

The Simple Solution

I watched a client's website, which had experienced flat growth for five consecutive years, increase its organic traffic by 8,745% and conversions by 272% within nine months of applying the principles explained in this chapter.

Another site generated a 75% conversion rate on its product pages when visitors engaged with their Q&A.

When conversion experiments or A/B split tests incorporate behavioral design principles as the testing hypothesis, they can produce positive conversion results 60% of the time. We have seen this for ourselves: A single test based on a single behavioral design principle on the home page alone produced a 41.14% lift in site-wide conversions with a 99.55% confidence interval.

The moral of this story is that a behavioral science-based approach to the online user experience can have dramatic effects.

At Shopper Approved, a reputation management service for ecommerce, we have found that online success often requires a proven and replicable system backed by science that can compound growth by creating more quality traffic to your site and a higher conversion rate on your site.

In this chapter, you will learn about these successful case studies, a new approach to growth called "the conversion path," and why this new science-based system is the most powerful framework for analyzing and optimizing the entire buyer journey, from search to checkout.

You will also see how applying just three behavioral design principles has created compound growth by generating more traffic and conversions for ecommerce websites.

These three principles are:

1. Pre-suasion
2. Social proof
3. Authority

You will also learn how these proven behavioral design principles work within the conversion path, as explained in our groundbreaking book "Reputation King," available on Amazon or at ReputationKing.com, where you can download a free digital and audio copy.

The Silent Killer

Friction is the silent killer of conversion. The first and most important thing an online marketer should do to improve their sales revenue is identify all the friction points on the conversion path and then do everything they can to remove or mitigate them.

Even if someone wants your product and is motivated to buy, there comes a point where too much friction kills the motivation. Statistically, 98% of website visitors don't convert to a sale, which gives you an idea of the impact friction has on your revenue.

Friction comes in many varieties, including:

- Lack of trust in the website, the transaction or payment security, or the product itself
- Fear of loss, failure, or embarrassment for making the wrong decision
- Too much effort or time to find the right product or complete the transaction
- Lack of clear value or benefits
- Can't get their questions answered quickly, easily or accurately

And here's a secret that very few marketers are aware of: Two types of fear or uncertainty must be addressed and overcome:

- The fear that the brand or product will not deliver the desired or promised result.
- The user's fear about not having the skills, time, or ability to execute or use your product correctly to get the desired result.

How many brands are aware of and clearly addressing the user's unconscious fear of failure?

The fear of loss (spending their money but not getting the desired result) and the fear of failure (not being capable of using the product or service properly) are far more potent as friction not to proceed than the hope for gain if everything worked as advertised.

To learn more about friction as an online conversion killer, read the book "Friction" by Roger Dooley, a leading ecommerce expert, speaker, and author.

Backed by Science

The conversion path model is scientifically different from the typical buyer's journey. The latter identifies and maps the sequence and steps to a sale but does not apply scientific methodology to analyze the friction points or optimize the journey by applying and testing the appropriate behavioral science principle for each step.

By contrast, in the conversion path model, we engineer into every step and point of engagement the appropriate sequence and application of one or more behavioral science principles for the web, from search to checkout, making the conversion path an integrated ecosystem of ethical persuasion.

Another rather revolutionary concept behind the conversion path is that in our model, we integrate, address, and optimize organic traffic (SEO), paid traffic (PPC), and conversion optimization (CRO) by leveraging these scientific principles.

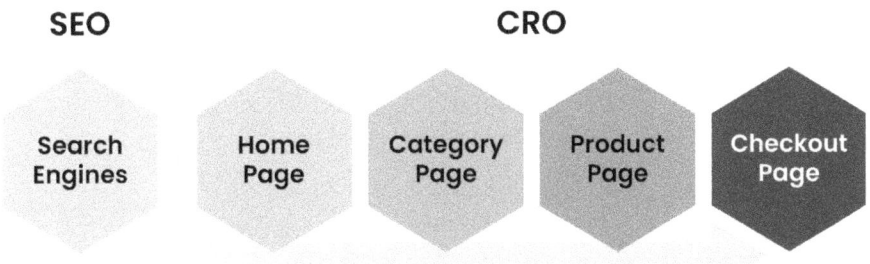

The Conversion Path begins with Pre-suasion in search and applied behavioral science principles at every step of the journey

The above graphic shows that pre-suasion occurs in search, while influence occurs throughout the journey, from search to checkout.

The common mistake made by most ecommerce sites is to treat paid traffic, organic traffic, and conversion optimization as separate, siloed activities executed by separate teams or agencies that do not communicate or work cohesively to consider the entire user experience as an integrated whole.

Pre-suasion

Pre-suasion is possibly the most potent single persuasion principle because it catalyzes all other influence principles when the shopper enters the journey with a more positive and hopeful viewpoint of the seller and the product solution. Yet, it's probably the most overlooked and least talked about principle within the arsenal of behavioral design principles.

According to Dr. Cialdini, Pre-suasion is "...science-based evidence of not just what to say to persuade but also when to say it." (Cialdini, Pre-Suasion, 2016, P. 12)

Pre-suasion is based on the following fundamental principles of psychology: how we frame and position information and how context and sequence are critical, allowing all other communication and persuasion strategies to work more effectively:

- **Receptivity:** Before introducing a message, you benefit by making your audience more sympathetic and receptive.
- **Salience:** Focused attention on a specific attribute or element of a message can cause the recipient to emphasize its importance and be more receptive.
- **Sequence:** What we present first and the context or environment in which it is presented (the precursor) changes how others perceive what we present next.
- **Pre-framing:** This allows you to shape someone's thinking and perception about your message, company, or product before experiencing it.
- **Anchoring:** The first data point, price, option, or point of comparison presented becomes the mental anchor against which all the following information or options are compared.

For these reasons, pre-suasion helps create the optimal sequence, context, and environment for persuasion principles to work better.

Understanding the persuasive power of sequence and pre-suasion, we have deliberately engineered it into the conversion path from the very beginning of the online search results all the way to checkout. This creates an integrated and cohesive ecosystem of behavioral design focused on building trust and authority.

Social Proof

Social proof is a powerful persuasion mechanism because it embodies several very pervasive psychological principles: System one thinking or mental shortcuts (automatic and easy decision-making), herd psychology, tribalism, and belonging (justification + survival instinct).

Social proof can be displayed in several ways. Still, it's most commonly delivered online through ratings and reviews like seller ratings, product reviews, and video reviews. In fact, Google calls reviews "the gold standard of social proof."

> *"Social proof fuels decision-making shortcuts. Ratings, reviews, and reputation fuel social proof."*
>
> –Nancy Harhut, Author of "Using Behavioral Science in Marketing"

Authority

When a company, website, or individual possesses and displays relevant expertise, they also gain more authority. The key is to display signals of expertise and authority correctly at the right time. This can be done through trust badges such as:

- Awards
- Recognition
- Review milestones and widgets
- Exclusive memberships
- Endorsements
- Certifications
- Degrees and training
- Published books
- Other accolades that suggest expertise in the field
- Years in business Milestones
- Evidence of popularity, expertise, or demand (speaking, publishing or podcast appearances, for example)

Becoming a topical authority and expert can be a very important aspect of pre-suasion and influence because experts are naturally more trusted and respected, and their opinions may reduce the fear of making the wrong decision.

We also proved our hypothesis that top search results carried more authority. Based on a national survey of 600 US adults, we found that

80% of consumers perceive the top organic search results as more authoritative.

During an exclusive interview at his research lab on the Arizona State University campus, Dr. Cialdini also supported our research when he stated that: "authority may come from the top organic search results and review stars that appear in search."

In short, Google is the most popular and generally regarded as the most authoritative search engine. Therefore, results displayed at the top of a Google search are consciously or subconsciously seen as the most trusted and authoritative resources.

When these page-one search results also contain review stars in the rich snippets, they possess the double-barrel effect of authority and social proof.

The Conversion Path

The first step of the Conversion Path is where pre-suasion begins, which is most often the online search results.

You must succeed here to establish yourself as a trusted and authoritative brand. Otherwise, your ability to drive high-quality, bottom-funnel, high-purchase-intent traffic will suffer, and the traffic you get will be more skeptical and less likely to convert.

In search results, first impressions, context, environment, and system-one thinking create the initial preference for a message, brand, or product, and getting this right is essential to your online success. As the saying goes, "You never get a second chance to make a good first impression."

The Search Results That Influence Pre-Suasion

The top search results include several aspects that can pre-suade more people to buy, including reviews and answers to the user's search questions.

Ratings and Reviews in Search

This means that search results with positive reviews across multiple review platforms can create a fertile environment for either persuasion or skepticism if those results display negative reviews or no reviews at all.

Q&A in Search

Getting the answers to your shopper's questions at the top of the organic search results is also critical. The fact is that people primarily use search engines to get answers to their questions. And if your answers to the product, brand, competitive, or service-related questions can consistently dominate the top search results, then you will automatically generate more high-quality, high-purchase intent traffic.

If you can do this at scale, with the help of an AI-powered and search-optimized Q&A tool, you can capture far more revenue-generating traffic for a much higher ROI than paid traffic.

The quality of the search results. Search listings are highly influential when they contain third-party social proof in the form of review stars in the rich snippets or when the search results are displayed as featured snippets that contain specific answers to searchers' questions. Featured snippets, for example, in position "0," typically get 35% of the clicks, giving you the highest possible chance for traffic and sales.

The position of the search results. According to research by Backlinko, the top 5 organic results (not including a featured snippet) get nearly 70% of the clicks.

The quantity of the search results. The more page 1 search results a brand or product generates, the more visibility and perceived "popularity and authority" they have, which means more opportunities to drive high-quality traffic to their site.

Our Unique Pre-Conversion Process

To leverage these criteria for influential search results, we have developed a process and software tools to optimize the pre-suasion phase of the buyer journey. This creates higher-quality and more trusted search results that visually stand out with review stars, featured snippets, and video thumbnails, leading to more visible, relevant, and higher-converting clicks.

Conversion Path Strategy for Search Results

Our strategy is to get you as many page-one search listings for your brand, product, competitive comparisons, and product questions and answers as possible. We accomplish this through various integrated tools and strategies, including seller ratings, product reviews, video reviews, and AI-powered, search-optimized Q&A.

Imagine your seller, product, and/or video reviews appearing in multiple page one results, including:

- Your website
- Your Google Business Profile (formerly Google My Business)
- BBB
- Shopper Approved certificate
- Trustpilot
- Sitejabber
- Walmart
- Facebook
- YouTube
- Google Shopping
- Google and Bing Ads
- Video tab search results
- Shopping tab search results
- Reviews tab search results

Also, imagine your product, category, and brand questions and answers appearing in the featured snippet or the top 1-3 organic search results.

This combination of top search results effectively gives you a search domination strategy.

Conversion Path Strategy for the Home Page

We conducted a national survey to test the idea of placing various aspects of social proof above the fold on the home page. We hypothesized that people spend milliseconds on a page determining if they like and trust the site before bouncing, so we had to convey trust instantly without scrolling.

What we found was that 73% of the survey respondents preferred the home page variant with the "Trust Bar" (see below), which displayed the rating, the review stars, and the percentage of customers who recommend the site (3 points of social proof), compared to the same version without these trust attributes.

We then tested the idea on an actual client website, which generated a 41% site-wide conversion rate lift with a 99.5% confidence factor. For the next test, we added a second component below the hero image, and we saw an additional 5% lift for a total 46% conversion increase.

This is now a conversion widget we offer that automatically and dynamically updates the review count and rating. It's just one example of how we test a behavioral design hypothesis with a survey followed by an A/B split test and then build software to power it.

Example of the Trust Bar

In addition to the Trust Bar at the top of the home page, we close the loop by offering seller rating widgets for the home page and a footer seal, creating a sandwich of trust signals and social proof.

Familiarity + Trust On The Product Page

The behavioral design principle of familiarity states that people feel more comfortable and confident in a familiar environment or situation. This principle extends to a website's user experience (UX).

We took this to heart and looked at the standard product page components of the most popular and successful marketplaces, including Amazon, Walmart, Home Depot, Lowes, Best Buy, and more.

What we found was a consistent use and placement of product reviews, Q&A, and, often, a website security seal across these marketplaces, creating a familiar and trusted user experience on the product page.

So, we created a hypothesis and tested this observation in another national survey.

We found that 91% of those surveyed preferred the product page example with these familiar elements to the example without. The image below represents the survey example, which is what the most successful marketplaces do, and what we have in turn built to replicate these marketplaces to maximize the principle of familiarity and conversions for our clients. We call this "The Traffic and Conversion Suite."

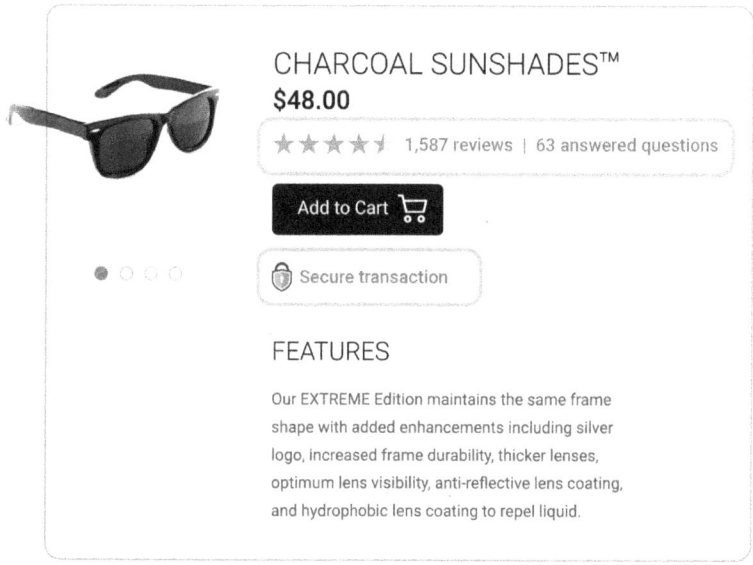

Image of the Traffic and Conversion Suite as displayed on a product page

Website security is also a powerful trust signal. Conversion Fanatics, a conversion optimization company, conducted a series of A/B split tests of the Trust Guard security seal on their clients' websites. They found that when the Trust Guard seal was present on the product page, regular orders increased by 19%, recurring orders increased by 28%, and the average order value (AOV) increased by 71%.

This is just one example of how a popular but critical trust badge can significantly improve a website's revenue by increasing trust and leveraging the familiarity principle.

Clients who used the Traffic and Conversion Suite have reported a doubling of their business, while others have reported significant conversion results, including a 75% product page conversion rate on one, and a 272% and a 380% conversion lift on others.

Summary

The top-ranking content in organic search is often perceived as the most authoritative and trustworthy by the consumer, even more so when it is adorned with review stars and lots of reviews. Therefore, the top five search results are the most trusted and authoritative and receive 69% of the clicks and traffic.

According to Google, reviews are the gold standard of social proof. They also create more trust and credibility for the associated product and/or brand, setting up the sale using the principle of pre-suasion.

Together, top-ranking search results, combined with review stars, create more pre-suasion in search, which transfers to more influence on the website when the proper trust signals and user experience are present.

This combination of pre-suasion in search, fueled by social proof and Q&A in the top search results, plus reviews, Q&A and security seals on the website, helps to create more trust, authority, and familiarity, which has proven to drive up to 8,745% more organic traffic and 272% more conversions.

Properly displaying and syndicating social proof and trust signals, on-page and off, combined with an AI-driven, search-optimized Q&A tool, improves search results and conversions, operational efficiency, and reduces traffic and Customer Acquisition Costs (CAC).

It's Your Turn – Get The Free Book

To claim your free copy of Reputation King, including 228 pages of strategies, research, examples, best practices, split test results, and case studies, supported by 91 color graphics, images, and examples, you can download the digital and audio copy at ReputationKing.com

DUANE "DJ" SPRAGUE
https://EvolveGlobalPublishing.com/s/duane

About the Author: Al Fabon

Al Fabon's journey as a Filipino leader, speaker, trainer, coach, and facilitator underscores the remarkable influence of unyielding passion. His experience is one-of-a-kind, as he moved from a conventional job in the public sector to a purposeful existence devoted to mentoring, coaching, equipping, and motivating people. In his unconventional journey, he has inspired many audiences across the Philippines. In pursuit of his unwavering dedication, he seeks to make positive and sustainable contributions to the world, a mission he has been carrying out for the past twenty years. He is resolute in his mission to shape and support the development of future leaders. With unwavering determination, he ignites the potential in others, encouraging them to pursue greatness and cultivate a positive impact on those they encounter.

He dedicates himself to speeding up his clients' progress, showing his steadfast dedication to guiding them towards achieving their goal. Through his facilitation, training, speaking, and coaching, he leads his clients on the path to realizing their full potential. By leading values-based leadership workshops, he helps his clients in identifying and clarifying their values for effective self and team leadership. He shares his knowledge and skills on influence, leadership, diversity, equality, and inclusivity. He tailors his coaching approach to address the ever-changing needs of his clients, guaranteeing their success in reaching their desired objectives.

Al's commitment extends to various aspects of his life. His overarching goal is to help his clients tap into their complete potential and excel. He devotes his energy to hosting training and workshops that guide people in uncovering their interests, strengths, and overall purpose. He fosters a safe space for them to explore various possibilities, engaging in thought-provoking conversations, and listening to their perspectives. His commitment to the youth is a beacon of hope, inspiring them to believe in their potential, motivating them to have faith in their abilities, and make impactful transformations.

Al was recognized as the Best Chapter President (over 100 members) by the Philippine Institute of Environmental Planners (PIEP) in 2021. He received the Life Achievement Award at the DILG NCR PRAISE Pagtanaw awards ceremony in May 2024.

Chapter 2

Give More First

by Al Fabon

Amidst fierce competition, ethical influencers will flourish and thrive. They are industry leaders who want to shape a more desirable world. Are you actively working towards becoming an influential person and shaping a better world? Today is the best time to develop yourself if you want to become a respected and influential leader.

In this chapter, I will share personal stories to illustrate how I achieve incredible results through ethical influence practices. I hope they add value to you. If they do, I want you to apply them in your own context so you can achieve transformative change.

Serendipitous Encounter

I was born and raised on the island of Banton, in the province of Romblon, Philippines. Growing up, the island lacked continuous electricity. The limited electricity supply in the town proper lasted for three hours each day, starting from dusk and ending in the early evening. During those few hours on weekends, we made the most of the opportunity to delight in watching movies in a handful of homes where we could watch "Betamax" films for a nominal fee.

When I was nine years old, I had the chance to watch a film that depicted the heartwarming story of a compassionate boy rescuing a girl from harm. He expected nothing in return, but the girl's family gave him a life-changing favor. The movie depicted the Filipino concept of *utang na loob*. It means feeling the need to repay someone for a good deed. It was my first time encountering Dr. Robert Cialdini's rule of reciprocity in a motion picture. In his book, *Influence: The Psychology of Persuasion*, Dr. Robert Cialdini explains, "The rule says we should try to repay what another person has provided us."[1]

The film had a profound impact on me. I was so captivated by the film that I envisioned myself as the protagonist, reliving every scene and line in my mind. I found myself lost in that daydream more times than I could count. However, I realized such narratives are few in actuality. As a young boy, I resolved to focus on how I can make it my reality instead of fantasizing about those movie-like narratives happening to me. I redirected my attention towards becoming a better person; a gift that people want to have.

Be the Gift

During my short stint as a college instructor, I gifted my students with an equal starting grade of 100% on the first day. My intention focused on instilling in them the confidence to pursue and attain their academic goals. I was the first one in the classroom who trusted their abilities. However, the students faced many challenges that hindered them from achieving the goals they have set for themselves.

I gifted struggling students with a performance conversation where I mentored and coached them. I encouraged them to consider different ways to achieve their goals. Of those who followed their action plans, 66% showed significant improvement and earned a passing grade by the end of the semester.

During the midterm, I asked my students to write anonymous feedback and submit it to me. Reading the feedback was like unwrapping a present. My heart melted when one student disclosed feeling jealous about those who were involved in the performance feedback sessions. This prompted me to invite both the top-performing students and those who require additional help in a performance conversation.

In addition, I took advantage of silence as a gift for my students, who need time to think before they can respond. During recitations, I allowed my students to reflect. Providing a learning environment where learners feel safe is as important as asking the right questions. When I reviewed the student absences, the results were surprising! The combined gifts resulted in reduced student absences by 30% in the second quarter, 40% in the third quarter, and 50% in the last quarter.

After graduating from college, a few students invited me to be their wedding sponsor. Some invited me to be a godparent to their children. There were former students who carved time out of their busy schedule for a dinner and coffee to catch up. Some invited me to travel together with them and their families. These and other invitations that I get from my former students are but a few examples of how they responded to the gifts I have shared with them. The relationship transformed from teacher to student; to becoming friends; and then from friend to a family.

I went to the United States of America to attend a conference in August 2024. When a former student learned about my travel, he offered to let me stay at his house with his family, which I accepted. He arranged his schedule for my visit and took time to tour me around several destinations across different states in the US.

During my stay, I got to know him better, his wife, his two adorable kids, and their friends who spent time with us over dinner. We recalled our time together inside the classroom and how much has changed and has not changed for us. It was an unforgettable experience and filled with pure joy.

I had the chance to tutor my cousin who attended high school during my time teaching at the university. Her mother would seek my help, and I accepted the role and enjoyed the journey. Today, my cousin works in the US and during my visit, he and my aunt took time off to spend some time with me. We explored Los Angeles, California;

we went to Disneyland Park, and took a speedboat adventure in San Diego, California. It was for me an exceptional adventure! My students reciprocated beyond the classroom setting long after the teacher/tutor-student/tutee relationship had passed.

Be a Leader Who Gives More First

Before becoming a team leader, I was an individual contributor. As such, I observed how other leaders led me. I etched in my heart the values I wanted to remember, including the practices and behaviors I wished to carry out whenever my time to lead came. Being an individual contributor taught me valuable lessons which shaped the leader I aspired to be.

During my time as a former middle manager in the public sector, I made use of my gifts to serve others. My role was to make the jobs of both my supervisors and direct reports easier and more efficient while achieving our common goal.

I often ask my supervisors, direct reports, and colleagues this gift-oriented question: "In which area do you need my help?" I view my skills as a gift to share. This question often receives a positive response. They inform me of the tasks they need to share with me and those they want to delegate to others, which leads to improved productivity and early submission of outputs. This gift-oriented question spread among my team members, which led to us achieving better results.

In 2021, when my supervisor noticed my personal laptop exhibited some problems, she offered her laptop, which was given to her by the office. I declined to accept it as I had intentions of purchasing a new one for myself. Upon learning of my plans to buy a new one, she suggested splitting the purchase cost, but I quickly dismissed the idea. When she saw the new laptop on my desk, she insisted I accept her share from her own pocket. She stated she wanted to contribute 25% of the purchase price of the laptop. She shared that she wanted to ensure I have my preferred laptop instead of any random laptop.

My supervisor acknowledged our extra efforts to achieve our common goal and responded in an encouraging manner by sharing the purchase price of the laptop.

As a leader and middle manager, I made time to coach my direct reports. I started by identifying and clarifying their values and engaged them in an intentional conversation. I asked them how I could better lead them around their values, understand how they show up at work, and why they behave the way they do. These are intangible gifts I gave them to show them their growth was important. In return, it has provided immeasurable benefits to all the team members. I knew we gained results when we won as the best performing field office for two consecutive years since its launching in 2022.

In June 2018, we established a local chapter of a professional organization. During the first couple of years, the chapter had less than 200 members. In the third year, we committed to growing our members. As such, we offered immersive organizational culture experiences as a gift to prospective members. We hoped such gifts would attract others to join the organization. Regardless of whether we had one participant or many, we persevered through all the activities as planned and they all paid off, thanks to all our members and volunteers who committed their time and efforts! Today, our chapter is one of the biggest chapters of the organization.

In 2021, we partnered with an organization and offered a free online course as a gift to prospective and new members. All our efforts gained results with a staggering 54% increase in membership in 2021 and 86% in 2022.

In the same year, we joined forces with ShareTree, Inc., an Australian social enterprise, to carry out a culture engagement survey. According to the report from ShareTree, Inc., our chapter's culture engagement outperformed the global average. Our score stood at 3.90/5 or 78%, compared to the global average of 3.69/5 or 74%.[2]

Servant leaders are those who serve for the benefit of their people and the organization. Choose to become a servant leader who gives more first.

A gift is not a reward

No matter what, a gift is always free. Service or product providers offer free services or products to provide prospective clients a taste of what they offer. In marketing, they call it a lead magnet. A lead magnet is a free product or service provided to the public to build a new relationship. It can come in different forms. It can be a book chapter, a quiz, free products, free speaking engagement, free training, or a free workshop, among others.

In order to showcase the difference I make in the training industry, I offer workshops as a gift to clients. I design free training workshops as a fresh experience for prospective participants. The free training gives my prospective customers a sneak peek into what I offer, and it also shows who I am as a trainer.

Give your products or services as a gift so your audience can experience what you offer. When you do, you can create a community of users whom you can turn into future customers.

At the conclusion of a project, I submit the draft output as a gift for my clients. I dedicate time to design the project output to make sure it adheres to the client's branding requirements. As a result, I often receive invitations from clients to work on more projects.

One time, I made a speaking packet which I gave to prospective clients. It gave me some results. Unsatisfied, I resolved to prepare a customized proposal to every prospective client besides the speaking packet. The outcome led to the closure of twice as many speaking engagements.

Be a Prayer Warrior

Giving a gift does not mean a person needs to spend money. I reach out to my social media followers, asking them to send me their prayer requests, if they have any. Those who are experiencing challenges send their prayer requests. To respond, I carve out time to pray and send the prayer to the person who requested it. Others return the favor by telling me they prayed for me as well! Imagine a community of people praying for me because I prayed for them first.

In September 2023, I posted a message in my Facebook account and I concluded it with an action item where I encouraged the readers to send me their prayer requests. A former student sent a message asking me to pray for her to pass the National Council Licensure Examination (NCLEX) of the United States of America. I prayed for her and sent her the prayer. Five months later, she sent a message thanking me with a photo showing me the favorable results of the examinations.

Build Better Relationships

My sister and her family paid for a visit to Manila for a brief vacation in June 2023. Per my recommendation, we had a family dinner at my preferred restaurant. As the dinner was coming to an end, my brother-in-law inquired how often I visit the place. I informed him I used to frequent the restaurant, although not in the recent past.

He inquired, "But why do the servers treat you like they know you for a long time?" I told him with a smile on my face that I make time to converse with the dining staff to build better relationships. Building better relationships is beneficial for everyone. When we treat people around us with respect, they appreciate the gesture and treat us extraordinarily well.

I once asked my friend to accompany me to a convenience store to get some necessities. Unbeknownst to me, he kept a close eye on me throughout the time I shopped and interacted with the store assistants and the cashier. After finding ourselves inside the car, before departing the location, he confided in me, saying, "Now I understand why you have such an extensive network. I noted how you spoke and treated the store assistants and the cashier. You spoke to them as you spoke to us, your closest friends."

I thanked him in return for noticing. I responded by saying: "We need to treat everyone with respect because everyone deserves to be treated as such." When we give other people our best self, they reciprocate and show their best self as well. By giving individuals the gift of respect first, we contribute to creating a community of respectful individuals. It is important that we practice it every day because when we do, we influence others and we contribute to nation building.

Travel with a Mission

Practical experiences provide the most impactful means to unlearn, relearn, and learn. That's why I make time to travel, exploring unfamiliar destinations and immersing myself in diverse cultures. Through my personal experiences, I have found strangers who opened doors to unique opportunities that extended beyond casual conversations.

In August 2019, I was checking in for my early morning flight from Singapore to New York. The flight had a four-hour layover in Dubai. I smiled and thanked the ground crew member who handed me my boarding pass, mentioning her name displayed on the nameplate she wore. When I mentioned her name, her eyes lit up. After about ten steps away from the counter, I looked back at her and I saw her still looking at me as I proceeded to the boarding area. We both smiled at each other.

I proceeded to the check-in counter and stayed until the boarding announcement. When the boarding gate opened, the boarding staff called the passengers for a systematic check-in. I belonged to the last group of four passengers to board the plane. During my turn, the ground personnel walked to the left of the counter and picked up my boarding pass. When he handed my new boarding pass, he smiled and said: "You're flying in a different zone!" Someone upgraded my seat to a business class! I beamed with joy as I walk to the plane door and to the stairs, heading to the business zone until I sat on my seat.

The experience left a lasting impression! I sensed that the last minute change of my seat occurred because of my treatment of the ground personnel, whom I addressed by her first name. Addressing a person by their first name is also a gift for other people. This demonstrates that you acknowledge the person's presence, and that person matters to you. Remembering someone's name is a skill we can all learn. There is a benefit to addressing someone by their first name without asking when they are wearing a nameplate.

In June 2013, I found an Apple iPad 2 buried in the seat pocket of an airplane. The iPad had a broken screen but works just fine. I tried looking for the person whose identity appeared on some of the accessible booking records saved on the iPad. Apparently, the owner didn't have a social media profile. I figured the person would create a social media account in the future and I would find him soon.

Fast forward to 2017, I found him on Facebook! So I sent a message informing him I found his iPad, and it remained in good condition. I wanted to return it to him as the rightful owner. Apologetic, he informed me he has no recollection of ever meeting me, so I clarified we hadn't and that I was attempting to identify the owner of the iPad I discovered. He admitted he was indeed the owner of the iPad. He thanked me for attempting to find him.

According to him, if I decided to return the iPad, we could meet in October. We met in November 2017, marking four years since I discovered the iPad. We met at a coffee shop. Upon expressing gratitude for returning the iPad, his first remark indicated his surprise at its weight, exclaiming, "Oh, this is heavy!" The iPad was owned thrice by the rightful owner: at the time that he purchased it; when he left it at the train station in Brazil and recovered it; and when he left it in the seat pocket of an airplane and I returned it to him with a brand new screen. The unexpected experience allowed us to build new friendship, which continues to the present day.

Volunteer

In 2011, 11% of school children in the Municipality of Banton were malnourished, either underweight or severely underweight. To help the school children achieve good nutritional status, I launched a donation drive in December 2011. I asked people within my sphere of influence to take part in the feeding program. I sent out messages using Facebook messenger, Facebook group, and through email. The message had the names of those who had sent their donation, and I updated the list to inform the prospective donor. Those who replied provided meals for a malnourished child for a month. I received favorable responses and achieved 68% of the target!

When I delivered the meal bags in January 2012, I had the chance to speak on behalf of all who partnered with us as donors. Tears streamed down my face as I delivered the message, witnessing the sad reality of malnourished children. It was heart-breaking.

To ensure the program reaches all the remaining 32% of target children beneficiaries, the school workers introduced a new food preparation technique incorporating a mix of local root crops. The result was the successful provision of a nutritious meal to all the intended child beneficiaries each day for more than a month, resulting in healthier school children! Many studies show that improved health among children is linked to higher rates of school attendance, lower dropout rates, and improved academic performance.

To our surprise, a local legislative resolution was put forth in October 2012, acknowledging and commending us for carrying out the feeding program. We felt a deep sense of gratitude upon receiving the unexpected recognition. We found the opportunity to help, and we joined the movement to build a better community where every child has equal access to proper nutrition. The local officials responded in kind to the contributions we made for the malnourished children, as stated in the resolution.

Looking Back, Moving Forward

The impact of the story about the compassionate boy on me was profound. It inspired me to become a better son, sibling, friend, coworker, leader, influencer, and human being. Thus, I exerted extra efforts to become a better person.

I encourage you to take action with what you have learned from the stories I shared. Implementing it in your context will yield profound impacts on your clients and the larger community.

May this be the spark that ignites your transformation into a valued and influential leader in your field!

As a speaker and trainer, Al strives to influence his audience to translate their insights into actions.

As a facilitator, he leads his audience through values-based leadership activities, helping them identify, define, and align their core values to effectively lead themselves and inspire others.

As a young leader, he is driven by a mission to empower the next generation to realize their full potential.

Bibliography

1. Cialdini, R. B. (2021). Influence: The Psychology of Persuasion (New and Expanded). New York: Harper Business.
2. ShareTree, Inc. (2021). Culture Engagement Report for PIEP NCR. (Version 4.3)

AL FABON

https://EvolveGlobalPublishing.com/s/al

About the Author: Maria Maier

Maria Maier is a dynamic leadership coach and organizational development expert with a deep passion for empowering leaders and teams to achieve their full potential. With an MBA and certification from the Maxwell Leadership organization in 2020, Maria has committed herself to helping individuals and organizations facilitate growth and transformation. She is also a Cialdini Certified Professional, having partnered with Dr. Robert Cialdini, author of Influence: The Psychology of Persuasion, to become a Founding Member of the Cialdini Institute.

Maria's expertise in ethical influence and leadership development has positioned her as a trusted coach and consultant to executives, driven professionals, and high-performing teams. She has worked extensively with governmental agencies, educational institutions, and corporate leaders, offering tailored programs that foster leadership qualities, enhance performance, and create lasting, positive change.

Maria's career began in the Mayor's Office of Volzhskiy, Russia, where she served as Chief of Staff, driving structural reforms in City Hall and launching a housing program that benefited thousands of residents. After immigrating to the U.S. at age 24, she spent over a decade in higher education, bridging gaps between trustees, donors, students, and faculty to enhance organizational effectiveness. Her journey reflects a profound commitment to intentional living and empowering others to thrive.

Building on her extensive and diverse leadership experience, Maria founded Step Up & Thrive LLC, a NYS and NYC WBE-certified business providing Executive Coaching, Leadership Training, HR and Labor Management Services, and Youth Leadership Development with world-class programs and resources. The company's mission expanded through a partnership with Vizient, Inc., enabling the delivery of strategic HR solutions to healthcare institutions across New York.

Maria is a dynamic public speaker, accomplished trainer, and trusted consultant who partners with entrepreneurs and executives to unlock growth and potential in their teams and organizations. She champions the belief that leadership isn't a position—it's a mindset. Through impactful keynotes, workshops, and team-building sessions, she equips leaders with the tools to elevate their influence, drive results, and achieve transformative success.

As President of the CNY BizTalkers and a board member of the Mohawk Valley Businesswomen Network, Maria combines her expertise with a passion for fostering out-of-the-box thinking and professional growth. Her mission is to empower leaders to embrace bold strategies, cultivate high-performing teams, and position themselves and their organizations for unparalleled success.

Maria lives in Central New York with her husband, Jeff, and their four children: Victoria, Peter, Robert, and Katrina. She enjoys a fulfilling career while being fully involved in the joys of family life.

Chapter 3

From Adversity to Abundance

by Maria Maier

The Alchemy of Adversity and Ethical Persuasion

"Fall down seven times, stand up eight," states a Japanese proverb. This was exactly the case during the USSR Perestroika era when a sixth-grade student declared her desire to transfer to a school with a profound study of English on the opposite end of an industrial city in the southern part of Russia. That 6th grader's idea seemed totally crazy and didn't get any approval from her parents due to a lack of financial resources and public transportation issues; however, she was determined to make it work. She insisted on switching schools and following a dream of mastering the English language as she convinced her parents, with her grandmother's support.

That student was me, and I fell fast from a hero to zero, from a high honor student in regular school to a complete dummy in English school. It seemed like a long nightmare with bad grades in English Basics, English literature, where we read and translated the original Shakespeare's "Romeo and Juliet", as well as Technical Translation. This became my reality over the next few months. It was quite a devastating journey, and I thought I was on the way out after multiple principal's warnings… until things began to change for the better, and my grades slowly improved.

I started taking private lessons with a tutor who believed in me and saw something in me. I learned a year later that my grandmother saw my determination and emotional struggle as she learned about my studying until 3 AM and offered my English tutor some vegetables and fruits from her dacha (summer cottage) to thank her in advance for a little extra time she could find to boost my belief and confidence in pushing through.

My dream about living in an English-speaking country was born as I finally felt like a fish swimming in water. I finally got it and started speaking 6th-grade English. My success was initiated by my Grandmother Nina's "Ethical Magic", the art of influencing positively while maintaining integrity and trust as she applied the powerful principle of influence called the Reciprocity Principle. Of course, none of us knew about its existence back then. However, this principle truly outlined my trajectory beyond my wildest dreams.

As I delved into the science of persuasion, I embraced the six research-backed principles as both a student and practitioner. These principles, including Authority, Social Proof, Scarcity, and Commitment and Consistency, became instrumental tools that I employed to facilitate desired change and effectively drive results for our clients.

The Clean Slate Philosophy and Ethical Influence

Reflecting on the profound impact that my English tutor, Aliah Shihamedovna, had on my life, it's clear that her willingness to adjust her schedule and provide lessons was more than just academic support - it was an embodiment of The Clean Slate Philosophy. Her belief in my potential allowed me to start with a 'clean slate', free from the constraints of past expectations. This philosophy of beginning anew, coupled with a nurturing environment, not only improved my grades but also instilled a newfound confidence that propelled me forward.

As I embarked on my career path, I carried with me the lessons of The Clean Slate Philosophy. The city of Volzhskiy with a population of 350,000 people faced the promise of industrial progress, and I found myself at the threshold of an extraordinary opportunity. Hired to work within the prestigious walls of the City Hall while diligently pursuing my Master's degree in Business Administration, my journey was marked by a challenging beginning. Two years in, I was promoted to Chief of Staff in the Mayor's office, a role that would challenge me like never before.

Amidst the seasoned ranks of municipal officials, I stood as the youngest, a fact that did not escape me as I navigated the complexities of leading significant meetings and demanding comprehensive reports. The challenge was not merely administrative; it was also a test of character and connection. It was in the genuine rapport I fostered with the directors of pivotal departments—Finance, Economics and Development, Architecture, and Civil Services—that I found the keystone of my approach.

To establish effective, mutually beneficial relationships, I discovered that the first step was to cultivate a genuine affinity for the leaders themselves. My demeanor was unfailingly friendly, polite, professional, and positive. This strategy, rooted in the Liking Principle, became the bedrock upon which I built my success. It was this very principle that enabled me to spearhead a monumental project - the launch of a subsidized mortgage program to make housing more accessible for the city's residents.

The trust placed in me by my superiors was evident when the First Deputy Mayor, Victor Ivlev, would call upon me to stand in for him during Open House sessions in the face of unforeseen emergencies. At the tender age of 23, to represent the City Administration and address the concerns of our citizens was an honor of the highest order. Whether it was environmental pollution from the industrial sector or grievances regarding noise from a new dental practice in a residential building, these encounters were revelatory, urging me to adopt a diplomatic and compassionate stance.

It was the Principle of Unity that guided me through the labyrinth of stakeholder feedback, enabling me to synthesize a solution that not only supported my boss's directives but also resonated with the hearts and minds of our residents. This narrative is not just a recollection of past achievements; it is a testament to the power of ethical influence and the indelible impact of leadership.

In the realm of ethical persuasion, the Clean Slate Philosophy played a pivotal role in the successful launch of the subsidized mortgage program in Volzhskiy. By embracing the principles of ethical influence, I was able to approach each interaction with municipal officials, strategic partners, and stakeholders without preconceived notions, allowing for fresh perspectives and innovative solutions to emerge.

"Ethical Magic" lies in creating genuine connections and fostering collaboration.

Navigating New Horizons with Integrity

As I navigated the complexities of a new chapter in my life, crossing oceans and borders to the United States, the ethos of integrity was my guiding star. Starting anew in a foreign land presented a kaleidoscope of challenges, yet it was the very essence of change that invigorated my spirit. Embracing the Liking Principle once more, I sought to forge connections in this unfamiliar terrain with the same genuine warmth and respect that had served me well in my homeland.

In 2004, as I embraced my new life in the United States, I found myself living out my childhood dreams. I arrived with a vision to start a family, be a devoted wife and mother, and continue my professional journey. The transition was not without its challenges; I was in a foreign country, without the comfort and support of family, childhood friends, or colleagues—and with only my husband and his parents by my side.

Yet, within a month, I was fortunate to secure a position at a local college, where I once again employed the Liking Principle to cultivate genuine connections and build lasting relationships with my new colleagues in the U.S. based on mutual respect and shared goals.

My approach was and still is simple yet profound: to like the person first. This philosophy enabled me to navigate the cultural nuances and establish a successful career while resonating with colleagues and students alike. It was through the application of these universal principles that I transcended barriers, inspired change with integrity, and found a sense of belonging in a world far from the one I knew.

As I started my American career in higher education, I got to interact with trustees, special donors, administrators, students, professors, and alumni and successfully continued to break invisible boundaries and close communication gaps.

I enjoyed working with students during the production season, commencement, or with alumni during reunion weekends in different administrative roles on campus; there was the particular process of co-creation that harnessed the Principle of Unity. Ticket sales and student engagement went through the roof as the Principle of Unity in our marketing efforts prompted students, professors, staff, and alumni to say "yes" to attending the performance out of feelings of togetherness or shared identity.

As I reflect on my life's journey, I'm reminded of the power of change and the importance of embracing it with integrity, no matter where you are in the world. My move to the United States was filled with challenges, but by genuinely connecting with others, I built a successful career in higher education. This approach to forming relationships, based on the Liking Principle, helped me navigate through unfamiliar territory.

However, my story took a dramatic turn during what should have been a simple dental check-up in Russia. Due to unforeseen circumstances, I had an MRI instead of an X-ray, which revealed something unexpected in my brain. The technician, using her authority without a doctor's evaluation, informed me of the discovery that would shift my outlook on life and my young family's future. It was a brain tumor.

This experience became a pivotal moment in my life. It underscored the fragility of our plans and the importance of living with intention. After a successful surgery, I emerged not only tumor-free but with a renewed sense of purpose and a heightened awareness of the value of each moment. These are qualities that I bring to my clients now, along with a dedication to fostering a culture of collaboration and excellence. It is the same spirit I brought with me to Russia in 2020 when the opportunity to deliver a training seminar for young entrepreneurs presented itself in my hometown.

My career at Hamilton College, where I bridged the gap between administration and academia, was fulfilling. However, I always felt the drive to do more. This drive led me to pursue further education in higher education administration, a journey that was halted by the global pandemic. Nevertheless, my commitment to personal and professional growth remained unwavering as I embraced change, the value of continuous learning, and the power of a supportive community.

After volunteering to do several training programs with my colleagues at Hamilton College and seeing the positive outcomes and great feedback from the participants, I realized my WHY had outgrown my job, and on December 30, 2021, my LLC was officially registered. In January 2022, I left Hamilton and jumped into the entrepreneurial world. With the help of the lessons that I learned from John Maxwell, Paul Martinelli, and Dr. Robert Cialdini, I rapidly grew my client circle.

When an opportunity to join a mastermind group with Paul Martinelli presented itself, I couldn't miss it. I wanted to meet the man who founded the John Maxwell Company, built many other multi-billion companies, and was behind the voice on the Thinking Partner faculty calls. It was during these mastermind sessions that I learned about the launch of the Cialdini Institute and my appreciation for the opportunity to join Dr. Cialdini's Institute as a founding member and become a Certified Cialdini Professional and Coach expanded.

Ethical Influence in Action: Case Studies and Principles

By sharing personal stories and international experiences, I am presenting real-world examples that illustrate the power of ethical persuasion in the professional realm. Working closely with high-performing professionals and HR directors, I've witnessed firsthand how Dr. Cialdini's principles of influence can be harnessed to foster not only business growth but also to enhance employee engagement.

The case studies will delve into scenarios where these principles were applied with finesse and integrity, leading to outcomes that benefited everyone: the individual, the organization, and its people. For instance, by leveraging Unity, we created a sense of shared identity and purpose, which is essential in aligning individual goals with the company's vision. The principle of Liking was used to build rapport and trust, making collaboration more effective and enjoyable.

Commitment and Consistency were key in establishing reliable patterns of behavior that reinforced the company's values and objectives, while the principle of Authority ensured that decisions were respected and followed through. These stories will not only serve as a testament to the effectiveness of ethical influence but also as a guide for you to implement these strategies in your life and organizations.

By facilitating two regional seminars with a franchise chain in Pennsylvania and Ohio, focused on specific strategies, we were able to drive results that benefited highly successful world-class professionals and helped them gain new levels of awareness around business growth.

It was the Principle of Unity activated by localism (since the majority of them were from the European part of the world) that allowed us to achieve the desired outcomes for business owners who had moved to the US after having extremely successful careers and outstanding performance records.

As I engaged in the conversations with the attendees after our training sessions, I learned that although they were equipped with tools and systems to run the *"business in a box"*, some of them struggled to launch their business, grow their book of clients, and attract and retain talented instructors. It was the application of the principles grounded by science and ethics that set the groundwork for us to discuss the strategies for communication and increase individual leadership capacity.

Working with the Crystal Clear Financial Group and its partners, including NY Life, has been a transformative experience, particularly around leadership development. By integrating long-term training focused on the principles of influence, we've seen a remarkable impact. This collaboration has allowed us to delve into the nuances of ethical persuasion and its application in financial services. The result? A strengthened leadership framework which not only enhances decision-making and strategic thinking but also permeates every level of performance. For example, after taking a deep dive into the Authority principle, new financial professional Anna was able to establish authentic connections in her geographic area by leveraging the power of introductions. This resulted in a 30% increase in client base within three months, 20% improvement in strategic decision-making and collaboration. This fostered a deeper sense of connection and trust across teams, enhanced overall performance, and positioned the company for sustained growth and success in the competitive financial services industry.

Patrick Lencioni says, *"the greatest competitive edge an organization can have is teamwork."* Most organizations aren't willing to take the time, energy, and money to do that. We were invited to partner with various organizations, helping them bridge communication gaps and foster a culture of collaboration and inclusion through Leadership Roundtable sessions and other effective team-building activities. As we deployed such principles of influence as Commitment and Consistency, Authority, Liking, and Social Proof, the results in the area of employee engagement and employee retention skyrocketed: participation levels rose by 85%, 90% reported feeling more connected to their peers, reducing feelings of isolation, with 50% improvement in teamwork and mutual support.

Reflecting on the past year, one of my private clients, Melissa, came to me for coaching while navigating the HR job market. Through a tailored coaching approach that includes a Coach Laboratory — where I provide additional valuable resources to expedite desired outcomes — we focused on Dr. Cialdini's Commitment and Consistency principle. By applying this principle strategically, Melissa not only reduced her job search timeline by 50% but also increased her interview success rate by 70%. Within just four weeks, she secured multiple job offers and ultimately landed her dream role.

We have also seen a great positive impact and ripple effect of the Reciprocity principle, which can include providing information, trust, some advice, or complimentary coaching consultation. These gifts were unexpected and meaningful in the form of either a complimentary coaching session, a book on leadership, or a complimentary training session. These offers in return yielded positive results and allowed us to secure contracts. Our piece of advice for you: when considering giving a gift, think about its significance and whether it's unexpected. This combination can greatly amplify the effectiveness of the reciprocity principle.

Our work with youth both in secondary and post-secondary education has been quite successful, and we believe the key to this success is the principle of Liking, which states that people like doing business with people who like them and are like them.

Working with college students and high school students is always fun and we start our interaction with the unspoken message "I like you!" This creates a positive energy and judgment-free zone with a professional approach.

One recent example was working with a group of international students who immigrated to the US and were in the Upward Bound Program as first-generation students getting ready to attend college. The group was very diverse and shy at first, however, we combined the Liking principle and Unity principle, centered around getting actively involved in co-creation, and amplified the sense of "we-ness" or togetherness. We made a point and emphasized co-creation among all students. This approach yielded remarkable effects.

Now, you might be wondering how to execute this in real life in the most effective way. The answer is simple: ask for advice. Often, when seeking partners or ideas, we tend to ask for opinions or help. However, if you simply ask for an opinion, it can create an opposite response of "us versus them". It separates people into "you" and "me," rather than fostering a sense of unity or "we-ness."

When you choose to ask for advice, it triggers collaboration and turns into a collective effort. Looking back at my student supervisory role, I managed to attract the best individuals to engage in co-creation by utilizing the principle of Unity that was amplified by asking for advice. This allowed me to effectively create partners in the co-creation process as I not only asked for advice but intentionally looked for advice on what to do or how to proceed.

Our recent certification as a Women Business Enterprise opened doors to network with national providers, including the healthcare improvement company Vizient. In exploring the opportunity to partner, we applied the principle of Social Proof, which suggests that we make decisions based on the actions of others. By sharing client testimonials and a proven track record of success, we are excited to move forward with this partnership.

The Ripple Effect of Mastering Ethical Persuasion

Bill Gates once remarked, "I was lucky to be in the right place at the right time. But many others were also in the same place. The difference was that I took action." This sentiment perfectly encapsulates the genesis of my foray into the realm of influence and persuasion. It was an honor to be invited as a founding member to participate in the launch of the Cialdini Institute, where I became one of the first certified professionals in this field.

I vividly recall a powerful quote by John Maxwell at the first International Maxwell Conference that I attended: "Leadership is influence, nothing more, nothing less." This resonated deeply with me and bolstered my commitment to aiding my clients and various organizations in unlocking new leadership horizons. The journey into ethical influence and the science behind it offered a profound avenue to broaden my business and enhance the entrepreneurial, career, and organizational endeavors of my clients.

Drawing from my diverse career experiences in Russia and the United States, I've observed firsthand how individuals often ascend to leadership roles based on their title rather than their readiness to embody leadership in their actions. They become IN authority rather than AN authority. Such circumstances can precipitate a cascade of negative outcomes, including diminished morale, subpar employee retention, and lacklustre productivity.

Sociologists suggest that even the most introverted among us will influence an average of 10,000 people throughout our lifetimes. Our influence extends to our spouses, children, relatives, neighbors, and colleagues daily. Hence, when I encounter individuals who dismiss the importance of leadership training, claiming, "I am not a leader; I don't care about leadership," my typical response is to challenge their perspective. I ask if they ever need to persuade or influence those around them. LinkedIn's research corroborates the significance of persuasion, ranking it as one of the top five most sought-after skills in today's professional landscape.

The transformative power of ethical persuasion has been a constant in my life, from my early days in Russia to my current role as a coach and a business consultant with innovative solutions. The mastery of this skill has not only propelled my personal and professional growth journey but has also been instrumental in the growth of clients that my company Step Up & Thrive, LLC serves.

Ethical persuasion is the cornerstone of effective leadership, and its power to create lasting change is undeniable. By mastering these principles, we can collectively harness the ripple effect of influence to foster harmony, diplomacy, and growth, empowering both yourself and others to achieve meaningful goals. The principles of influence are at the heart of our Ethical Leadership program, equipping professionals to lead with integrity and inspire positive transformation within their teams and communities. At Step Up & Thrive, our mission is clear: we coach and train high-performing professionals and partner with HR leaders to drive results that elevate your organization, your people, and your success. Together, we can create a future where your leadership leaves a lasting, impactful legacy.

Visit us at https://stepupandthrive.com to discover how we can help you, your team, or your organization unlock unparalleled growth while leading with influence and integrity.

MARIA MAIER

https://EvolveGlobalPublishing.com/s/maria

About the Author: Vladimir Bushin

As the visionary founder of the Negotiation Practice Community, an Influence Coach certified by the Cialdini Institute, a Camp Negotiation Systems Coach, and the author of an acclaimed rapport-building course, "7 Levels of Nurturing"™, Vladimir stands at the forefront of empathetic negotiation and ethical influence.

Vladimir is also a Founding Member of the Cialdini Institute, certified trainer of Crucial Conversations, and "The Best Relationships Builder" award winner of the TNC World Negotiation Competition 2024.

His negotiation journey started with reading "Start with NO" by Jim Camp in 2005 and includes over four years of mastering negotiation and Crucial Conversations training, coaching, and consulting, enriched by many years of corporate leadership.

Vladimir's effectiveness as a negotiation and influence coach is underscored by his direct impact. He has successfully trained dozens of professionals and coached hundreds of individuals in developing their communication skills. Under his stewardship, the Negotiation Practice Community has grown to hundreds of dedicated members.

Driven by a mission to unlock the potential within every leader, Vladimir endeavors to transform how individuals engage, resolve conflicts, and build trusting relationships in the business and corporate world.

Aside from his coaching practice, Vladimir is an avid reader, constantly seeking to deepen his understanding of human interactions. His zest for life extends to windsurfing and hiking.

Chapter 4

Liking is King

by Vladimir Bushin

The challenge:

"My senior partner doesn't support me. I must complete my scientific report, but I can't do it without his help. He doesn't reply to my emails, he doesn't meet with me, and he doesn't give me his valuable advice. I'm stuck!"

My client, Chelsie (names are changed for privacy), seems desperate. She can barely contain her disappointment and frustration.

"Was it different before?" I asked.

Chelsie said working on her first PhD-related report was a collaborative team effort. But they clashed over who would be the first author. Despite her significant contributions, her supervisor listed himself first and put her in second place, to her great surprise.

It felt utterly unfair and disrespectful of all the hard work she put in. She prepared all the data, did all the analysis, organized the chapters, and created all the graphs and images.

"Why would my senior partner or anyone else be mentioned before me?"

She couldn't tolerate this obvious abuse of her talent and sent an email explaining how wrong this was and that she deserved the first position because, effectively, it was her report.

"I felt oppressed by this narcissistic person. Seniors don't understand equality. Therefore, I felt I had to fight for my rights.

And I won! They agreed to make me the first author. But later, I found that my senior partner was a bit withdrawn. What can I do now?"

Stories like that are very common. Cold relationships slow down progress, cause project delays, and bring them to a complete halt. They destroy opportunities, undermine reputation, and lead to professional isolation. They cause rework, ineffective solutions, and negative feedback. Overall, they decrease revenue and increase costs.

What is at the root of all cold relationships? What's the "elephant in the room" you see clearly, but my client didn't acknowledge?

Let's look at a similar issue in a different context to understand it better.

Jerry is a junior military lead. He is ambitious, organized, focused, and determined. He wants to move up the ranks.

Unfortunately, he's developed a cold relationship with his peer, which has started to impact his results. His peer is more senior and has worked in his role for over 10 years. He is experienced but doesn't seem to pull very hard.

Recently, Jerry was assigned to lead a project and given a team where all members reported to this peer. Since then, the project hasn't gotten much momentum because the team members do not have enough time to work on it.

It started to feel like his peer had assigned the lowest priority on this project for all his direct reports. It didn't sound good for Jerry's reputation and ambitious plans.

"Tell me more about your peer," I asked him.

"Well, he is a strange guy," Jerry started. "He comes to work late, is not very responsible, takes vacations very often, doesn't ask much from his people, and doesn't seem to be very clever!"

Jerry said it with visible irritation.

"Do you respect him?" I asked.

"Honestly, I don't."

"Does he know about it?"

"I guess he might know because we had conversations before where I encouraged him to try a bit harder."

Let's stop here and think: what's the biggest problem in this story?

That's right. It is disrespect between 2 parties that are independent and free to make decisions.

Respect:

If they didn't work in the same organization, they'd probably never talk to each other. They'd create a distance far enough to avoid any contact. However, because they are working in the same structure and given a common goal, they will deal with it by putting minimum time and energy into helping each other.

Disrespect is the primary reason why relationships turn cold. It goes against one of the most basic principles described in Dr. Cialdini's book, "Influence, The Psychology of Persuasion." It's the principle of Liking. People do business, collaborate, and like those who like them. And they will avoid those who don't.

In business, Liking means money. It will make the difference between winning or losing contracts, being promoted or losing the job, and getting invited or being forgotten. Imagine how important it is to make the most of this principle!

When it comes to choices, Liking is King.

In this chapter, we'll see how the principle of Liking relates to Respect and how to build a path from negative relationships into positive ones. We'll see examples of how people use the principle of Liking to obtain free services, build businesses, and improve sales.

Let's start with the foundation for success with any goal involving people – Respect.

Safety

The word "Respect" comes from the Latin "Respecere," meaning "to look back". In modern English, it has evolved to mean holding someone in high regard or esteem, acknowledging their worth, and giving them proper attention and consideration. Therefore, Respect means Regard.

Here's the key question:

If someone likes you, will they disregard your feelings, interests, and values? Will they disrespect you as a person?

Of course not.

People who like you will also respect you. They won't hurt you and will care about your safety, comfort, desires, principles, and interests. It is safe to be around people who like you.

What can you tell about people who don't like you?

They probably won't care about your feelings, won't notice your boundaries, and won't regard your interests, dreams, and hopes. They won't worry about your financial future and your success. It's unsafe to deal with them because they may disrespect you as you are not important to them.

Have you been in similar situations?

Conclusion #1: It's only safe to be around people who respect you.

There's another important connection that is worth mentioning. It's the connection between Respect and Fairness.

Fairness:

In 1982, 3 German researchers, Güth, Schmittberger, and Schwarze, created "The Ultimatum Game," which became well-known for testing human psychology. The rules of this game were simple:

In stage 1 of the Ultimatum Game, the first player proposes a specific split of a fixed amount of money, say $10, to the second player. In stage 2, the second player can accept or reject the proposed split. If the second player accepts, $10 is divided according to the proposal. Otherwise, both players get nothing.

The game's creators first assumed that the first player could keep it all, and the second player would be indifferent and accept any split.

The experiments have shown that responders rejected many offers and usually accepted only near-equal split proposals. More shocking is that the rate of rejections increased when the initial amount increased. Imagine that the $7 and $3 split has more chances to be accepted than the $70 and $30 split.

Many people would abandon $30 just to ensure that the unfair first player gets nothing. They were happy to pay $30 to hurt the unfair player even when they were offered a significant amount and could just say "Yes" to get it!

Why would the second player give up easy money? You guessed it – they are paying for fairness. The unfair split feels like a loss of self-worth. But there's no loss in the status quo. They prove that they matter.

The translation of "Respected" from the Russian language is "Important." "I respect you" sounds like "you are important to me" in Russian.

When the first player makes an uneven split, it sends a subtle message: "You are less important to me. I can disregard your interests."

The second player responds with a non-verbal "I'll prove to you that I'm very important" by refusing the unfair deal.

Most people turn down an unfair deal even if they lose the obvious benefits.

Conclusion #2: No business works outside of respect. Because disrespect is unfair.

Respect is like air for relationships. If you run out of it – you're done! Don't even try to make a deal because it will fail.

This resolves the dilemma between "fighting for what's right" or keeping respectful relationships. "Fighting" is about forcing your feeling of fairness on others regardless of the cost. Therefore, it's disrespectful. Even if you win once, you'll lose respect in relationships. And this is what happened in the first two stories.

Now, let's see how the principle of Liking solves these problems.

Trust:

Imagine a horizontal line. There's an extremely negative feeling on the left side of it – it's when people hate each other. On the opposite side – an extremely positive feeling when people love each other.

What's in the middle?

In the middle, people are OK with each other - a neutral state.

They won't mind you operating and doing your business beside them. But they won't necessarily want to help you. They won't want to harm you because they won't desire any negativity in relationships.

It's a place of mutual respect, and it is indeed a safe place. Golden middle.

Liking resides on the right side from Respect. Somewhere between Respect and Love. Therefore, when people like you, they also respect you. Being on the good side builds a feeling of safety and trust in your relationships. People will protect such relationships and invest in them.

On the other hand, if they disrespect you, they will be on the left side of the neutral state and somewhere between Hate and Respect. This is a risky place where they don't care about you and potentially dislike you.

When people feel disrespected, they become unsafe. They try to protect themselves and create distance from the source of disrespect. They try to avoid and disengage. Therefore, a "cold shoulder" and distancing are symptoms of disrespect and disliking.

How many times have you seen this?

Many people don't notice the issue or believe it lives on the other side. They only shrug their shoulders. Others try to fix it by "drawing a line in the sand" by sharing their feelings. Unfortunately, it may look defensive and self-centered.

But building Liking always feels friendly. It's inclusive, engaging, and brings more results.

Conclusion #3: Don't build Respect. Build Liking. It will be easier and will create safety and trust.

Bonuses:

A hidden benefit that will be lost in the face of disrespect is "discretionary goodwill." No one would think of helping someone who disrespected them. It would be unreasonable to voluntarily go the extra mile and support the success of disrespectful people. It's inefficient to support someone who will be acting against you and will disregard your interests.

There are more benefits to being in the "Liking zone."

According to the scientific research, one of them is the "Halo effect." People tend to assign many positive traits to those they like: honesty, kindness, intelligence, wit, and even physical attractiveness.

Another scientifically proven effect of Liking described in Dr. Cialdini's book is that we tend to forgive mistakes and explain them rationally when we like someone. At the same time, we give them full credit for any good deed without a question.

In the extreme form, we could call it "Blind Love" when people don't see the disadvantages of those they really like and assign them all the good traits.

Unfortunately, it works similarly on the negative side. It's hard to prove you're a good person if you have been put in a zone of distrust. Even the most generous and selfless acts will be questioned and given a rational explanation. At the same time, any perceived mistakes will serve as proof of your bad character.

Have you faced this before?

Negative perception will keep you in the zone of fear and risk. It will feel unfair and will sabotage the business. That's why professional negotiators address negative history before discussing a new deal.

Conclusion #4: If you have a history of bad relationships, address it before you get to any business. Restore respect and build Liking.

Getting out of bad relationships is a hard job. You'll need to activate all 7 Principles of Influence.

Let's start with examples of activating the principle of Liking, as it will be useful in every situation.

We are similar:

One of the activators of Liking is similarities. Surprisingly, even small similarities will work. They may include similarities in preferences, habits, opinions, body type, eye color, height, accent, outfit style, posture, and many other things. Many things may signal, "I'm like you".

For example, similarity in names could be one of the strongest sources of Liking. It's completely irrational, but it's true.

I had a client who wanted to purchase training from me but was not sure about my credentials. Committing your time and money is hard when you don't feel 100% confident about your coach. Later, my client revealed that one of the deciding factors was that the first 4 letters of our last names were the same. It gave my client a feeling that purchasing a product from me is safe and that I will stand behind my services. While I appreciated the trust and committed to satisfying all the expectations, I couldn't explain the reasons for moving forward with anything but the principle of Liking.

We naturally want to support and help people who are similar to us. Some similarities are not apparent. The good part is we can find similarities if we want to, even when we seem different.

The process of finding similarities activates the principle of Liking. If you're a consultant or advisor, it's crucial to find similarities because Liking is a decision-making factor. If applied early, Liking may double or triple your conversion rate.

Conclusion #5: It's important to show you are similar. People will be predisposed to do business with you. Do it early in the conversation.

I once travelled from the US to Egypt and had to change 3 planes. The website offered me a choice of seats for $30 on each plane. I thought I would save on it and prepared to get randomly assigned seats, which meant I would have to be confined in the middle seat on a 10-hour flight from Chicago to Istanbul.

But one conversation has changed it.

You are special:

I've always felt shy about talking to strangers, so I keep pushing myself to overcome my fears. When I arrived at the airport, I struck up a friendly conversation with the airline administrator behind the counter while checking in. I learned that she came to the US two months ago and likes it here. I also briefly mentioned I was an immigrant, too, and asked her if she plans to settle in America. I complimented her English teacher as she spoke very good English.

At the end of this short conversation, it hit me: "Why wouldn't I ask about the seats?"

"Will it be too much to ask of the window seats?" I said.

She had already printed my boarding passes but tore them down and discarded them. Then, she assigned me new seats and printed new passes. All for free!

What a gift! My 20-hour trip got instantly better with window seats on all 3 planes!

Conclusion #6: Making people feel important, showing respect, and mentioning similarities activate the principle of Liking.

The Principles of Influence work. These scientifically proven principles are practical, efficient, and, most importantly, they are true, natural, and wise. You recognize what people want and give it to them. And then you ask for what you need with all respect and responsibility. And you leave it up to them to decide. That's what Ethical Influence feels like.

Let's return to the stories of disrespect. How can you regain respect and liking if you end up on the negative side?

Credibility:

The issue on the negative side is that not only do they dislike you, but you also lose credibility. When people dislike you, they may think you don't have integrity, and you are self-centered. It's a bias. We can't do anything about it. It's human nature.

To overcome this challenge, you'll need help from a trusted third party to activate the Authority principle. You'll need to be re-introduced as a credible person, and it's best if your good friends speak about you and your positive traits and deeds. You can't do it yourself.

The problem lies in their vision of the future based on their past experiences. If someone doesn't like you, they'll expect future interactions to be negative, projecting their past stories into the future.

To build a new positive vision, they need to hear different stories. This is how people form perceptions. When they hear stories about somebody, they have similar experiences as if things would unfold right in front of their eyes. Stories form perceptions if they are told by trusted people.

One lady, let's call her Susan, worked at a large corporation with one of her colleagues, Ralf, who didn't seem to put too much extra effort into his work. He never came to work before 9 am. He would promptly leave at 5 pm. It seemed like he was aiming for the minimum effort he could make at work. It irritated Susan for months because she was sure Ralf was a slacker and didn't care about the company's success.

"He always puts his personal time above his work."

Susan once shared her concerns with her colleague, Grace, at a water cooler. What she heard from Grace surprised her. Grace told her that Ralf is raising 3 autistic children without a mother, and when he took his position, he agreed with the management that his family duties wouldn't be impacted.

This new information and the way Grace told it caused a transformation in Susan's perception of Ralf. She went to Ralf's office and apologized for her negative conclusion and attitude that Ralf might have felt. Ralf accepted the apology and thanked Susan for stopping by to talk about it.

Later, Susan heard a knock on her door. It was Ralf. He knew that Susan was working on an important report for the upper management and had heard of a recent conversation between the management and a client about a certain issue. He recommended Susan include information and a solution for this issue.

This short conversation allowed Susan to create an outstanding report and get compliments from the upper management. All of it was due to Ralf's advice and willingness to help Susan voluntarily. Note that if Susan hadn't changed her perception of Ralf, she may have disregarded his advice, thinking that Ralf was giving it out of his own interests. Ralf's advice wouldn't be as credible.

Conclusion #7: Start by activating the Authority principle to restore credibility. Ask a trusted third party for help.

Getting it back:

With credibility improved, get back to the "negotiation table" and restore fairness. Find the sources of mutual struggle. If anything signals disrespect or unfairness, what exactly is it? Figure it out. Make an agreement about respecting each other's boundaries.

Another important principle of influence from Dr. Cialdini will help. It is a principle of Reciprocity.

One of the principle's activators is concessions. When you agree to respect someone's boundaries, you can ask them to respect yours. That's the fastest way to restore respect and safety in your relationships.

As a next step, when you talk to the other side, remind them about your common goals and purposes, the years of working together, and other sources of Unity. It's another powerful principle that creates relationships. People who consider each other a part of something bigger, people who share identity and purpose, trust each other more.

You probably made commitments to support each other and collaborate when you joined a project or entered into a partnership. Reminding them about their commitments and expressing gratitude for them will activate the Consistency principle, which will bring up the reasons for supporting each other.

Finally, with respect restored and reinforced by Unity, Commitment, and Authority, the principle of Liking can be reactivated. Find similarities, compliment their work, communicate what you like about them, and make them feel important. This will define the turnaround in your relationships and restore the trust that is so essential for collaboration.

You can't lose when applying the 7 principles of Influence by Dr. Cialdini. They are bullet-proof principles, and Liking is one of the most impactful. People who like each other get out of their way to keep supportive relationships. They want to be liked and will give you reasons for that.

Like others first, and you will see the difference in your career, business, and life. It will start blossoming like a bush of roses in the hands of a skillful gardener. And the gardener is you.

Restoring respect may take some time because you'll have to find all the sources of discontent and agree on solutions. But everything is possible with the powerful Cialdini's 7 Principles of Ethical Influence, effective communication strategy, and proven habits of building a dialogue.

To learn practical tips about building business relationships and winning business, find free masterclasses, subscribe to a newsletter, and consider advanced learning programs at http://businessrelationshipscoach.com.

For further information about Dr. Cialdini and his work, please visit *http://cialdini.com.*

VLADIMIR BUSHIN

https://EvolveGlobalPublishing.com/s/vladimir

About the Author: Christian Younggren

Christian Younggren embarked on his automotive industry journey in 1992 at Mills Chevrolet in Moline, IL, following his graduation from Augustana College with a degree in Business & Psychology. Over the course of 13 years, he ascended through the ranks, starting as a Salesperson and progressing to roles such as Finance Manager and Sales Manager.

In 2000, Christian was selected to attend the prestigious NADA Dealer Candidate Academy, marking a significant milestone in his career. Subsequently, he assumed the role of General Manager at Mills Chevrolet, where he led a sales team that achieved record-breaking sales volume and customer satisfaction. His success in senior leadership positions laid the foundation for a transition into sales training.

Christian honed his sales training expertise with notable organizations such as Cars.com, GP Strategies Regional Training Manager for the Kunes Sales Training team, and as the Director of Business Development & Sales Training at Smart Auto Group. His journey led him to start his own sales training company, Kaizen Automotive Consulting, in 2019.

Renowned for his unwavering passion for learning, Christian is a founding member of the Cialdini Institute of Influence and is well-respected in the industry. Colleagues and clients praise his professionalism, exceptional coaching abilities, and engaging speaking skills. Beyond his dedication to sales training, Christian is actively involved in real estate management and has diverse interests, including martial arts, reading, and travelling with his family.

Chapter 5

The Experience Trap: When Too Much Sales Knowledge Becomes a Blindspot

by Christian Younggren

It was August Saturday afternoon at a Large Mid-West Chevrolet dealership, just shy of closing time, when a beat-up Ford truck wheezed its way into the dealership lot. It emitted a sigh of relief, as if it knew it was about to be relieved of its rusty burdens. A hulking, middle-aged behemoth emerged from the battered truck, his face obscured by a baseball cap struggling to contain his wild, salt-and-pepper mane. His beard had engaged in a turf war with his hair, and both were winning. His outfit screamed "laundry day? What laundry day?" with faded overalls clinging to dear life, a once-white t-shirt now displaying an abstract masterpiece of sweat stains, and boots so caked in mud they looked ready to sprout their own ecosystem.

In a move that would make a professional baseball player proud, he expertly aimed his stream of chewing tobacco spit into a nearby bottle. With the grace of a walrus on roller skates, he finally managed to extricate himself from the driver's seat, emitting a sound that could only be described as a cross between a groan and a battle cry.

The salespeople, usually a pack of eager vultures ready to swoop in on potential customers, were instead like tired lions at the end of a long day in the savannah, eyeing up the newcomer with suspicion, their minds already processing visual cues to judge if he was a serious, credit-worthy buyer.

Hank, known colloquially as "The Hammer," was particularly vehement in his disdain for the truck and its owner. "I'm not taking that guy," he declared with all the conviction of someone who believed they could smell bad credit from a mile away. "He's a credit criminal. Did you see the We Tote the Note sticker the tailgate? Let's get out of here... let the new guy wait on Mr. Overalls!" And with that, the pack scattered like startled pigeons, leaving Christian, the fresh-faced recruit, to face the music.

Next, Christian, with the confidence and sincerity of someone who had yet to be jaded by pre-qualifying by appearance and years of dealership politics, strode over to the man in overalls, extending a hand and a warm smile. "I'm Christian," he said, as if they were meeting at a local tavern rather than a new car lot. The man looked, and said, "I am Butch, Butch Jefferson."

As they sat down to discuss the man's vehicle needs, Christian couldn't help but take in Butch's appearance—Yes, he was a walking testament to the trials and tribulations of rural life—a man who had likely swapped stories with more livestock than people and had sampled more questionable chili at roadside diners than he cared to admit. But beneath the layers of grime and grease, there was a certain charm—a ruggedness that spoke of adventures in the heartland and a willingness to embrace life's messier moments.

As they delved into Butch's interest in new trucks and the ways he planned to utilize it, an unexpected camaraderie began to blossom between them. Despite their obvious differences in background, they found common ground in their enthusiasm for that gleaming, brand new Chevrolet parked outside. Before they knew it, they were back from a whirlwind demonstration drive, and after a mere 30 minutes of hashing out payment options, they found themselves seated at Christian's desk, penning the final paperwork to seal the deal.

As Christian affixed the plates to the freshly sold Chevrolet, a whirlwind of thoughts swirled through his mind like a tornado in a cornfield. In a world where Hank's seasoned car sales experience was supposed to be the golden ticket to success, how had it all backfired? And was it merely coincidence that his own lack of expertise in the field had somehow led to this unexpected triumph? He still did not grasp the intricacies of terms like "We Tote the Note" – whatever that meant. What would happen if he acquired the same knowledge and expertise as Hank and the gang? Would he, too, find himself sizing up potential customers before they utter a word? If they did not pass the eyeball test, would he soon be fleeing from potential customers like they had?

Christian couldn't help but wonder how he could ensure that his growing experience in the industry would not become a hindrance rather than an advantage. How could he maintain the fresh perspective that had somehow worked in his favor today, even as he became more entrenched in the world of car sales? It was a puzzle he knew he would have to solve, but for now, he allowed himself a moment of quiet triumph as he admired the shiny new Chevrolet sitting proudly on the lot.

Unfortunately, this is not a new or unique story. In fact it plays out time and time again in many retail sales environments. We all know, retail sales are a numbers game, right? The more sales opportunities, the better! We've learned never to judge someone by the way he looks or a book by the way it is covered, right?

So why does this scenario unfold so frequently in sales showrooms around the world? Are we simply lazy, disorganized, or caught in a haze of confusion?

In this chapter, we will delve into the psychology behind why The Hammer & Company ran away from a sale and how they tried to justify it in their minds. I will show you how you can keep this from happening to you.

Fast & Slow Brains

To truly understand what led these veteran salespeople to let a sale just walk by, we need to start by understanding how our brains process information. In the book "Thinking, Fast & Slow" by psychologist Daniel Kahneman, Dr. Kahneman explains that two systems govern our brains. System 1 is fast, intuitive, and emotional thinking, while System 2 is slower, more deliberative, and more logical. System 1 thinking often occurs automatically, without effort or conscious awareness, while System 2 thinking is more conscious and requires more effort.

Us humans would like to think we really think…but we don't think as much as we think, we think! We think that when it comes to making most decisions, we use the Slow Brain, especially for big choices that involve money, career, or significant life changes. We believe we rationally think through our options and choices with the slow, System 2 brain. However, Dr. Kahneman's research has found that System 1 runs the show 95% of the time.

It has been theorized that reliance on the Fast Brain stems from our ancestry, tracing back to our "caveman" days. We were wired to conserve energy—it's ingrained in our DNA! After all, thinking requires energy, brainpower, and effort. System 1 is geared towards conserving time and energy, so it instinctively draws upon past experiences to react to current situations. We rely on these past outcomes as shortcuts, allowing us to make guesses, hunches, and lean on intuition and emotions to navigate life's decisions. While these shortcuts often serve us well, there are times when they lead us astray—just like what happened to Hank and his friends.

So, it was the Fast Brain's whirl of rapid cognition that lead to a cascade of events to unfold on that Saturday, resulting in doubting Butch's willingness and financial ability to buy a car. For the remainder of this chapter, we will dive into each component. We will find out how the Say-Do Dilemma bred complacency, how Representativeness Bias and Confirmation Bias clouded judgment, leading to both character and financial missteps. Then, we will see how both the Authority & Social Proof Influence Principles compelled others to heed Hank's ill-advised counsel. Let us look at each of these.

The Say, Do Dilemma

One of the reasons Hank missed the opportunity for his third sales of the day is because he was a victim of his own success. After securing two sales earlier in the day, he became complacent and found justification in it. This is a classic example of the Say-Do dilemma. This is a counterintuitive mindset that seems to affect those whose paycheck is in the form of commission. When it comes to working on a commission, common sense would dictate the more effort expended, the more money earned. We often proclaim we will do anything to maximize our paycheck, yet our actions tell a different story.

In a 1997 study, this phenomenon was explored in depth in the "Labor Supply of New York City Cab Drivers: One Day at a Time" paper. It sheds light on why it's notoriously difficult to hail a cab in New York City on rainy days. The data looks at hours worked and income produced. Despite stating their long-term aim of maximizing profit, cab drivers were primarily driven by a goal of hitting their personal daily income targets. Their focus in the short term was on paying their taxi rental fees and knocking off early for leisure time even when they could have taken more fares. They are unknowingly anchored by this personal daily income target.

It's crazy...they often worked longer hours during slow business periods to meet these profit targets, yet paradoxically, they tended to quit earlier during high-demand times like during concerts, sporting events, or rainy days. Rational behavior to money would dictate the opposite strategy, wouldn't it? Wouldn't it make more sense to work longer hours when the demand was higher, and knock off early if no one wanted a taxi? This would help them reach their profit and leisure goal. This behavior reflects a focus on immediate income needs and time off were more important than long-term profit maximization. It is the infamous Say-Do dilemma in action, we say we want one thing, more money, but do another, like quitting early on a day when the rain creates more demand for taxis.

This phenomenon resonates with the current story, where experienced salespeople like Hank prioritize hitting their income goals for the day. Like the cab drivers, they may be inclined to call it a day after achieving their daily target, even if it means missing potential sales opportunities later in the afternoon. In the fast-paced world of sales, success is often measured by the latest achievement, leading to a constant drive to secure immediate income. Thus, the Fast, caveman brain instinctively prioritizes immediate financial needs and conserving energy, sometimes to the detriment of long-term success.

Representativeness & Confirmation Bias

In this story, Hank's actions also illustrate how cognitive biases like Representativeness Bias and Confirmation Bias, triggered by Fast Brain thinking, can impact decision-making in sales.

Representativeness Bias is a cognitive bias wherein individuals assess the likelihood of an event based on how closely it resembles similar events they have encountered in the past or how well it fits a particular prototype. In simpler terms, it is the tendency to make judgments or decisions based on stereotypes or previous experiences rather than considering all relevant information.

In the context of this story, Representativeness Bias is evident when Hank's Fast Brain quickly forms judgments about the customer based on stereotypes associated with the Buy Here Pay Here sticker on his truck. Instead of engaging in Slow Brain thinking, which involves deliberate and analytical processing of information, Hank relies on Fast Brain thinking, which is intuitive and automatic. This Fast Brain thinking leads Hank to make assumptions about the customer's financial situation and likelihood of purchasing a vehicle without fully evaluating the individual circumstances.

Furthermore, Hank's initial assumption triggered by the BHPH sticker is reinforced by Confirmation Bias. Confirmation Bias is a cognitive bias wherein individuals tend to seek, interpret, favor, and recall information that confirms their preexisting beliefs or hypotheses. In simpler terms, it is the tendency to look for evidence that supports what we already think and to dismiss or overlook evidence that contradicts those beliefs.

This bias causes Hank to seek out information that confirms his belief that the customer cannot buy, while ignoring evidence that contradicts this assumption. As Hank observes the worn-out Ford truck, overalls and scruffy appearance of the customer, his Fast Brain swiftly concludes the customer is not worth his time. Even when the customer drives a Ford truck to a Chevrolet dealership, Hank's brain jumps to the conclusion that "Ford people don't buy Chevys," further validating his initial assumption.

These cognitive biases prevent Hank from effectively evaluating each customer's potential as a buyer and lead him to miss potential sales opportunities. Instead of engaging in Slow Brain thinking and carefully considering all relevant information, Hank's biases cloud his judgment and limit his effectiveness as a salesperson.

Authority Principle & Social Proof

Additionally, the Authority Principle and Social Proof played a role in influencing the behavior of other dealership salespeople, further reinforcing Hank's actions. This is dangerous for the company. It can lead to lost business and, even more importantly, a poor reputation.

The Authority Principle is a psychological phenomenon wherein individuals are more likely to comply with instructions or orders from a perceived authority figure. In the context of the story, Hank, as a seasoned and experienced salesperson, holds a position of authority within the dealership. When he expresses skepticism about the customer with the Buy Here Pay Here sticker on his truck, his colleagues may defer to his judgment and follow his lead, assuming he knows best due to his authority status. This Fast Brain thinking leads them to adopt Hank's perspective without critically evaluating the situation themselves.

Similarly, Social Proof is a cognitive bias wherein individuals look to the actions and behaviors of others to determine the appropriate course of action in each situation. In the story, when Hank expresses reluctance to assist the customer based on his assumptions, his colleagues may interpret this as a signal that it's acceptable to do the same.

As Hank begins to gather his belongings to leave, other salespeople, even those who realize the assumption of poor credit might be false may feel compelled to follow suit due to the influence of Social Proof. Seeing a respected colleague like Hank dismiss the potential sale creates a social norm within the group, and there is a sense of peer pressure to conform to this norm.

This Fast Brain thinking leads them to conform to the group's actions without independently assessing the situation or challenging Hank's assumptions. The influence of Social Proof further reinforces Hank's Authority. Being considered an Authority, his actions influence the other salespeople from engaging with the customer, contributing to a missed sales opportunity for the dealership.

The combination of cognitive biases like Representativeness Bias and Confirmation Bias, triggered by Fast Brain thinking, along with the influence of the Authority Principle and Social Proof, leads the other salespeople to follow Hank's lead in dismissing the potential sales opportunity presented by the customer with the Buy Here Pay Here sticker on his truck. Instead of engaging in Slow Brain thinking and critically evaluating the situation, they rely on shortcuts and group dynamics, limiting their effectiveness as salespeople.

It can be difficult to effectively address cognitive biases like Representativeness Bias, Confirmation Bias, and the Authority and Social Proof Influence principles within the realm of sales because it requires one to learn how to balance experience and non-judgement.

To overcome cognitive biases like the ones Hammer and colleagues faced, one can employ several strategies:

1. Awareness and Training: The first step is to recognize the presence of these biases and understand how they influence decision-making. Providing training sessions that educate salespeople about various cognitive biases and their impact on sales interactions can help them become more aware of their own thought processes.

(For a Free 30 Performance Coaching session on Human Decision Making, go to https://www.kaizenautomotiveconsulting.com/)

2. Encourage Critical Thinking: Encourage salespeople to engage in Slow Brain thinking by critically evaluating each sales opportunity independently. Encourage them to ask questions, gather all relevant information, and consider alternative perspectives before making judgments.

3. Challenge Assumptions: Encourage salespeople to challenge their own assumptions and those of their colleagues. Just because a customer has a Buy Here Pay Here sticker on their truck does not necessarily mean they have poor credit. Encourage salespeople to approach each customer with an open mind and without preconceived notions.

4. Seek Diverse Perspectives: Encourage collaboration and teamwork among salespeople to gain diverse perspectives on sales opportunities. Encourage them to discuss and debate different viewpoints to ensure decisions are based on a thorough examination of all available information.

5. Leadership Role Modeling: Leaders within the dealership, including Hank, should lead by example by demonstrating open-mindedness, critical thinking, and a willingness to challenge assumptions. By modeling these behaviors, leaders can set a positive example for their colleagues and encourage them to do the same.

(For a Free 30 Performance Coaching session on Leadership Role Modeling, go to https://www.kaizenautomotiveconsulting.com/)

6. Create a Supportive Environment: Foster a supportive environment where salespeople feel comfortable questioning assumptions and challenging each other's perspectives. Encourage open communication and provide constructive feedback to help salespeople overcome biases and improve their decision-making skills.

By implementing these strategies, Hank and his colleagues can mitigate the influence of cognitive biases and create a more effective and inclusive sales culture within the dealership. This, in turn, can lead to better decision-making, increased sales opportunities, and greater success for the dealership.

In a whirlwind of Fast Brain thinking and snap judgments, Hank and his gang at the dealership found themselves caught in a tangled web of cognitive biases. With Representativeness Bias, Confirmation Bias, the Authority Principle, and Social Proof pulling the strings, they danced to the tune of assumptions and stereotypes.

But here's the twist: despite the Hammer and friends' expertise and experience, they fell prey to these biases, leaving them scratching their heads and wondering why the smartest salespeople stay dumb. The truth is intelligence alone is not enough to outsmart these sneaky biases. It takes a conscious effort to recognize them and a commitment to Slow Brain thinking to overcome them. We think we think, but we just do not think as well as we would like to...think! You must be humble enough to recognize that Fast Brain thinking and biases are tough to recognize.

So, fear not, dear reader, for there is a light at the end of this biased tunnel! By donning their critical thinking hats and embracing the power of Slow Brain thinking, Hank and his colleagues, you, or I can break free from the shackles of bias. We should challenge assumptions and seek diverse perspectives; however, the key is to create a supportive environment—one that lets open-mindedness reign supreme. Be curious, but without judgement!

In doing so, they will not only unlock hidden sales opportunities but also pave the way for a brighter, more inclusive sales culture. So, let us slow those brains down and learn to overcome biases, one sale at a time!

And remember, it's not about being the smartest salesperson in the room—it's about being the wisest.

CHRISTIAN YOUNGGREN
https://EvolveGlobalPublishing.com/s/christian

About the Author: Ellin Sidell

Ellin Sidell is the CEO of the Sidell Method, a boutique professional services firm in Talent Development with a proven track record in helping smart organizations maximize their human potential at all levels, from Leadership Influence Mastery and Strategic Mentoring Acceleration to Sales Team Enablement.

Ellin is a committed professional who is acknowledged for over thirty years of leadership and impact in a range of positions, including those involving global programs and project management, cross-functional solutions delivery, business and operations analysis, process-driven supply chain, and forecasting analysis. Her breadth and depth of experience inform her keen understanding of projects, processes, and technology, and above all, the people strategies needed to realize favorable outcomes. A persuasive communicator, thought leader, and team builder, Ellin is highly regarded as a tireless customer advocate and builder of lasting professional relationships who is results-driven with communications savvy.

Ellin's impressive career path has seen her build effective teams, systems, processes, and solutions that have grown multi-billion-dollar businesses for iconic companies such as Nestle, Microsoft, and Costco.

Instrumental in removing friction between Ops and Sales at Microsoft, Ellin delivered myriad multi-million-dollar IT initiatives, and established and optimized Retail Sales Account Manager processes for the $1B+ Xbox brand.

At Costco, Ellin founded a Leveraged Mentorship program that served over 200 mentees in five years and was recognized by both the Costco VP of Journeys and the then Costco CEO, Craig Jelinek. The program continues to this day.

Partnering with Dr. Cialdini, author of the bestselling Influence: The Psychology of Persuasion, Ellin became a Founding Member of the Cialdini Institute and is a Cialdini Certified Professional.

Ellin is an Associate Certified Coach (ACC) through the International Coaching Federation (ICF), a Certified Executive Coach through the Center for Executive Coaching, a Tiny Habits Certified Coach, a Maxwell Leadership Coach and DISC Consultant, awarded an Associate Neuroplastician (A.npn) certificate from the Organizational Neuroscience Network (ION), and a PMP (Project Management Professional) through the Project Management Institute. She holds various Agile certifications, such as Scrum Master (CSM) and Advanced Certified Product Owner (ACSPO).

Ellin lives in Bradenton, Florida with her husband, David Irons. She has two daughters, Kelsey and Marissa.

Chapter 6

3 Winning Influence Strategies in Fortune 500 Companies

by Ellin Sidell

Introduction

The summer after graduating college my corporate career was just beginning. I was bright-eyed and eager to make a positive difference in the world. A few decades later I would be introducing the CEO of the 12th largest company to the entire corporate campus at an event for a program I had founded. How had I got there? Through sheer hard work – every day. I shared my ideas, got people on board, and made real change – even in large Fortune 500 companies with their rigid processes.

Over forty years after my graduation, I discovered Dr. Cialdini's book, Influence: The Psychology of Persuasion. While reading, I had an epiphany. After decades of working in corporate America, I became proficient in applying these principles through trial and error. I'd helped grow multi-billion-dollar brands by applying these principles to three strategies: partnership, mentorship, and sponsorship.

If you had asked my younger self to imagine that SHE was destined to achieve all that, she would have been inspired. But all that hard work ... If only someone had taught those principles to me earlier on, imagine what I could have achieved. What I want to do is go back to that bright-eyed young woman to tell her the key to her success is to be herself and apply Dr. Cialdini's seven influence principles, and in doing so, gain her voice.

I can't do that, though. Instead, this is my gift to you. In the following pages, I am going to share my stories from three of the world's largest companies – Nestle, Microsoft, and Costco – in the hope you can apply the strategies I used similarly. Getting a Yes from others can help you achieve remarkable results in your career and life too. Whether you are a professional or a manager at any level in an organization up to the C-Suite, I hope you find value in these stories of the ethical application of influence to drive growth in your teams and organizations.

The Three Winning Strategies

There are three strategies you need to employ to ensure business success: partnership, mentorship, and sponsorship.

Here is how I define each of these terms:

Partnership is when you establish a key trusted relationship with one or more individuals, cooperating to get results. This does not have to include a legal arrangement. I have seen many people partner together in a variety of ways, including coaching, masterminds, and as team members. The etymology of the word "partner" means "one who shares power or authority with another.

Mentorship is a learning process between a mentee and mentor where the mentee drives the relationship based on their career and professional development goals. The role of the mentor has evolved, moving away from the "sage on the stage" to the "guide on the side". Accordingly, the mentor supports the mentee in reaching the mentee's goals via knowledge acquisition, application, and reflection. The etymology of the word "mentor" comes from the root, "men" – to think. If trust has been established, a mentor can become a thinking "partner" to the mentee.

Sponsorship happens when a leader advocates for you by using their social capital in a room you do not have access to, thereby creating pathways to increased growth opportunities, greater responsibilities, and potential promotions. The etymology of "sponsor" means "a surety or guarantee". Therefore, someone who sponsors you will possess a genuine belief that you can deliver on these increased responsibilities because they are risking their reputation by endorsing you. This endorsement is not based on favoritism but on trust in your abilities and potential for success.

Let us now look at the three success stories, through the lens of these strategies.

Nestle

It was the mid-90s, and I was a Forecasting Supervisor with the Nestle Petcare division. I was trying to calm my nerves because I was about to challenge my boss and advocate for implementing a new system he was against.

Leading the forecasting team, we had already streamlined processes and procedures, resulting in a saving of 52 analyst labor hours per month. In my view, we could not move the dial further on increasing forecast accuracy without advanced statistical models (Manugistics System). Notably, this was a departure from our manual forecasting method.

Sitting in his office, I told him we were going to have to "agree to disagree". My goal for this meeting was to get his approval to send the memo I had drafted to the President of the division. In the memo, I recommended that the president sponsor the Manugistics Systems project, which would allow us to uplevel our forecasting system and processes for the entire Carnation Company.

I watched my boss mimic the scene from the 1970s TV show, Kung Fu, where the master opens and closes his hand, revealing and hiding a pebble, challenging the other person to grab it. My boss was a quirky guy. I played along in many meetings over the time I reported to him but was always unsuccessful.

Ignoring the pebble this time, I took a deep breath and made my pitch. He said it was okay to agree to disagree and I should go ahead with my memo. Success! Chancing upon my victory, I threw my hand out and snatched the pebble for the first time ever. I was astonished, yet he smiled knowingly; he knew he had taught me well and that I was ready. The pebble I now held symbolized my readiness for more responsibility. In the TV show, the master says to young Caine, "Grasshopper, when you can take the pebble from my hand, it will be time for you to leave."

A few weeks later, I found myself entering the elevator with my 4-month-old daughter at the same time as Mr. Harris, the President. He said: "I got your memo." My anticipation rose. At this moment-of-truth, my daughter decided to try and unbutton my blouse to start nursing! My role as a mother had unexpectedly overlapped at this pivotal moment in my career, and now I was faced with a daunting 17-floor elevator ride. In a moment of inspiration, I shifted my daughter to my other hip to avert disaster. Then the President said: "I agree with you." I got a Yes! The rest of the elevator ride was a grueling battle of trying to stay engaged in an elegant conversation with the President while shifting my daughter from hip to hip in my attempt to stay clothed. I emitted an almost inaudible sigh when we finally reached the bottom floor of the building; I left the elevator telling him I would stop by his office for the next steps.

Sponsorship

The influence principle I used was authority. To be in a position where I could credibly influence the President of the division to say "yes" and sponsor the Manugistics implementation, I had to reduce his uncertainty by proving I was an authority (expert). In his eyes, the results I produced when leading the team to streamline forecast processes made me an expert on the subject.

As my career continued at Nestle, the President also became a sponsor for me because I had proved myself to be an influential problem solver. I like to think he might have been impressed by my multi-tasking skills in the elevator! Brent, my boss and mentor, was also a sponsor for me. Not long after the pebble interaction, Brent was promoted to Director and I was promoted to his vacated position, Manager of Production, Planning and Logistics. I suspect Brent recommended me to the President for the promotion. This is a great example of using the authority principle to gain sponsorship from multiple levels of leadership, and allows successful results to be seen and rewarded.

Mentorship

Brent was fun to work with. He came up with a "coin jar policy" – strongly advised but not mandatory – where he asked each member of his team to put a quarter into the coin jar for every minute we were late to a meeting. This was how he funded our team parties. Being a tardy man but one of integrity, Brent ended up contributing the most coins to the jar.

Despite all the fun we had, having my boss as my mentor was not without challenging moments. One October, he was more than forty-five days past the due date for my annual review, which was delaying my yearly merit increase in my paycheck. At first, I was frustrated, but then I got creative. I wrote up a "Notice of Delinquency":

WARNING: You are now more than 45 days past due. Your outstanding balance is *$15,480.00.

Prompt attention to this notice along with a generous merit increase will be taken into consideration in any settlement of this issue.

Note: This fee is based upon the previously implemented $0.25 coin jar policy charge applied to every minute that you have been late in giving Ellin Sidell her performance review. Due to the importance of this feedback, the $5.00 cap is not applicable.

Please return this notice immediately along with a suggested meeting time and place.

Thank you

Upon receipt of the Notice of Delinquency, he scheduled my review immediately. In this example, I used both the consistency and contrast principles, albeit in a humorous way. I was activating the consistency principle by reminding Brent of evidence of his previous words, i.e. the coin jar policy. I also used the contrast principle because my merit increase was much less than the coin jar delinquency balance.

Microsoft

If it wasn't for my successful influence on the President of Nestle Petcare and the subsequent Manugistics implementation, a recruiter using the Manugistics conference attendee list would not have called. Such is fate that I was able to learn about a Microsoft Forecasting Manager position, which I landed. This next story picks up seven years into my Microsoft career, after I had transitioned to IT as Solutions Manager.

My team was asked to rearchitect the $10 billion end-to-end Entertainment and Devices supply chain processes and systems. I was faced with this question: How can I get the project sponsor to endorse and fund a workshop to elicit requirements faster and more effectively than our current approach? This was another significant influence opportunity.

At this point in my career, I had over 45,000 hours of expertise in process improvement and reengineering across multiple companies and industries. I knew what it took to do this right, and we needed an innovative approach to not only create a long-lasting new supply chain process, but also to elicit the system requirements within the context of a flexible manufacturing, distribution, and fulfillment business model.

Partnership

My first step was to gain the agreement of Rudra, my partner whom I had been working with for many years. We used to describe ourselves to internal clients and engineering teams as two sides of the same coin. For any given project, Rudra was engineering-facing as the technical program lead, while I was client-facing as the business process lead. As such, we were demonstrating the liking principle because we were cooperating towards a common goal.

After I shared the research and findings with Rudra, he agreed that the next step was to present our joint recommendation to the project sponsor, Ken, the Director of the North America Supply chain.

Sponsorship

During the meeting with Ken, I explained our plan to expedite the project. The typical method of eliciting requirements through separate sequential meetings with the business stakeholders would take too long – potentially up to a year. Moreover, this approach may not have fully met the business's needs for a comprehensive solution encompassing an integrated business model, redesigned processes, and detailed system requirements.

Instead of the sequential (and traditional) approach, I proposed that we hire an expert in facilitated workshops to elicit requirements through collaboration, reducing this phase of the project to only months. I recommended Ellen Gottesdiener as the facilitator since she was well regarded in the industry, and had an impeccable reputation. Moreover, she literally and physically "wrote the book" on this best practice, Requirements by Collaboration: Workshops for Defining Needs. To further bolster my recommendation, I shared that I'd received approval for this workshop approach from key stakeholders, and provided Ken with their names.

I used two influence principles to lower the sponsor's uncertainty.

Social proof – by sharing the names of the key stakeholders in agreement with the workshop.

The authority principle – Ellen Gottesdiener was a best-selling author and expert in her field.

Rudra and I were excited when the project sponsor agreed to adopt this innovative approach. The workshop was a great success. We even received a vote of confidence from a skeptical business leader who told me that they were sold on implementing this new workshop approach for future projects!

The deliverables that came out of that workshop made it possible for the project to be completed in record time, with an ROI of at least $20 million over the eight years the system was in place. Not only did we produce an impressive ROI, we made the $10 billion Microsoft Entertainment and Devices worldwide supply chain more agile, adaptable, and aligned.

Costco

In 2015, I had been at Costco for a few years when I learned about a new one-on-one mentoring program under the Journeys group, and managed by the team responsible for corporate leadership development. The program was accepting applications. In the guidelines, it stated very plainly that the applicants would be considered on a "first-come, first-served" basis, pressuring me to apply immediately. With only thirty mentee openings, they had used the scarcity principle to motivate me (and others) to apply quickly. I was excited when I was accepted into the 9-month program.

During the program, I had the opportunity to meet senior leaders at Costco. The first half of the program consisted of senior executives sharing their Costco career stories and company culture with us each month. Then midway through the program, each mentee was paired one-on-one with a mentor.

My mentor was Teresa. In a life-changing conversation, I told her that some of the program leaders were saying, "Isn't it nice that you are meeting and developing relationships with your peers in the program?" I told Teresa that I was learning a lot and enjoying the program, but I was not meeting or getting to know the other mentees. There were some meet-and-greet sessions, but not sufficient time to overcome the awkwardness of being strangers and transition into developing true connections. We were also invited to presentations but had little time before or afterwards to mingle and network.

I told Teresa about a Leveraged Mentorship format I had learned from Susan Forney (deceased) when I was a co-mentor at Microsoft. I am so grateful to Susan who, with her infectious exuberance, taught me about the power of the transformation that can happen in trusted professional circles. Once I had explained the basic framework, program elements, and peer-to-peer relationship development to Teresa, she also saw the value and became a sponsor for me, and advocated for the leveraged mentorship format program to Sue, the VP of Journeys.

Sponsorship

A year after my involvement in the one-on-one Journeys mentorship program, I was still hoping to get Sue to approve my leveraged mentorship pilot. My final influence opportunity was not an elevator pitch, but a "salad bar line" pitch. Sue was ahead of me in the line and I said, "The Mentee Ring Program pilot will be complementary to your existing program. Don't you want to say yes instead of no to the other thirty or forty applicants you do not have room for in your one-on-one program?" That was the winning influence approach; she said yes!

In that situation, I used the liking principle since I was proposing to cooperate with her team to work towards a common goal. I also used contrast with the current situation of her team having to say no to around forty employees a year, when she could be saying yes.

Partnership

I became the founder and volunteer program manager of the leveraged mentorship program, which we named the Costco Corporate Mentee Rings. The success of the initiative relied upon the collaborative efforts of both volunteers and employees. I was fortunate to have exceptional partners, Lauren and Dixie, on the volunteer side. In addition, the unwavering support and commitment from Amy and Diane, Journey's Program Managers, were instrumental to the program's growth and success. In a five-year period, we expanded the program from seventeen participants to over two hundred, positively impacting many employees and leaders.

The Mentee Ring program would not have been a success without the partnership of the many people who served as mentors in the rings. There were over forty mentors during those first five years, and all wanted to help others grow. This was a perfect example of the unity principle in that they were investing into the "we-ness" of Costco as a whole, and its culture.

Another principle the mentors were using was the principle of reciprocity. They provided intangible gifts to their mentees: listening and supporting them in unexpected ways, tailoring their help to the mentees' learning goals and objectives, and providing meaningful perspectives.

Summary

Application of Ethical Influence in My Career

Through this chapter, I aimed to convey how I applied the principles of influence effectively, both in my career and within Fortune 500 companies, resulting in significant win-win outcomes. The thread of influence wove through my career, leading me from Nestle to Microsoft, then Costco, and now to my own firm.

When I think back to my younger self after graduation, I see I didn't realize how critical ethical influencing would be to my career. I helped build effective teams, systems, processes, and solutions that have grown multi-billion-dollar businesses and brands for some of the most iconic companies in the Fortune 500.

The Why Behind Leveraged Mentorship

Despite my success, there were times when my limiting beliefs – rooted in unresolved childhood embarrassment – held me back. It wasn't until my mentor, Craig, challenged me to "get uncomfortable" that, as a breast cancer thriver, I entered into a "Cancer Contest" – winning second prize – and I finally had my breakthrough moment. My prize was to cut a 30-second ad, inviting others to get early detection for breast cancer – but the point is, this is when I started to realize my voice mattered. I also learned that when we choose to use our voice to serve others – by paying it forward – then we serve ourselves as well.

As such, the "why" behind founding the Mentee Ring program was personal. With a heavy heart, I recognized that many of my colleagues had untapped potential and no mentor to help them. Many did not see themselves as leaders. I had several hugely transformational mentors who saw my potential even when I didn't yet see it. My mentors, along with these seven influence principles that I unknowingly used, helped me find my voice.

In 2022, my professional career as an employee ended, but not before the thrill of a lifetime. I introduced Craig Jelinek (then Costco CEO, now Chairman of the Board), to all the corporate office employees and that year's mentees, at a Q&A event for the fifth anniversary of the Mentee Ring program.

The Future

As the CEO of the Sidell Method, a boutique professional services firm, I have my sights on the future by helping and serving others.

Influence consistently ranks among the top skills sought by employers today. If my stories showcase what can be achieved through on-the-job acquisition of influence skills, just imagine the untapped potential that could be unleashed through focused training, practice, and the application of influence.

The practice of ethical influence, viewed through the lens of these three strategies — partnership, mentorship, and sponsorship — is undeniably powerful. Look at the opportunity that lies before us – to teach the principles of ethical influence to individuals and teams by having that influence training sponsored by corporate leaders.

Everyone wants a successful career – whether for themselves, their colleagues or their employees. Nobody should be left to figure this out on their own. A small investment in training and coaching will see each individual's career grow as they achieve success in their job. This success, in turn, adds value to the company's bottom line.

Imagine if company employees all knew how to leverage the ethical influence principles through the use of the 'Three Winning Strategies of Partnership, Mentorship and Sponsorship'. These strategies are something no one in corporate trains on, let alone in conjunction with the Cialdini Principles - so why wouldn't you want to be ahead?

Mentoring and coaching are my passions. Paying it forward is my calling. My firm exists to help smart organizations maximize their human potential at every level. We can teach influence to your employees so they may then add value to your company by living The Sidell Method motto: Don't Find Yourself. Define Yourself and Go Beyond!

ELLIN SIDELL

https://EvolveGlobalPublishing.com/s/ellin

Epilogue

You can't read a book in an hour. But here's the way to preview the most important lessons. In this chapter, you'll find the takeaways from the whole book, written by the authors.

Duane "DJ" Sprague

E-commerce Success Starts Here focuses on the fundamentals of online success by leveraging behavioral science principles within the e-commerce conversion path. Sprague introduces "pre-suasion" as a strategy to shape a potential buyer's mindset in the search results even before engagement on the website. Key insights include the importance of a positive first impression in search and the significant effect of trust signals, such as star ratings and reviews, and gaining the top search positions to create exponential growth.

Case studies and research demonstrate how e-commerce sites using behavioral design principles like pre-suasion, social proof, and authority experience enhanced traffic, conversion rates, and revenue.

The chapter also emphasizes reducing "friction" by offering answers to questions and addressing user uncertainties about the brand or product — to support conversions and foster growth through trust-building and confidence.

Al Fabon

Give More First highlights the profound reciprocal benefits that come from being the first to give thoughtful, unexpected, and personalized gifts. Through personal stories, Al shows how gifting others and expecting nothing in return can build meaningful connections, uncover opportunities, and create impact.

The chapter showcases real-life examples of different ways to give gifts in a variety of situations. Power points include: be the gift; be a leader who generously gives first; be a prayer warrior; build better relationships; travel with a mission; and volunteer.

This chapter will inspire readers to change their mindset and consider every interaction as an opportunity to add value to others through gift-giving. Readers can start their journey toward becoming a valued industry leader by translating the ethical influence examples in their context at the individual, team, organizational, and community level.

Unlock the impactful force of ethical influence with Give More First.

Maria Maier

Beverly Sills once noted that "there are no shortcuts to any place worth going," and this rings especially true on the journey of self-leadership and leading a team - it's often an uphill climb, full of challenges and moments of solitude.

In the chapter From Adversity to Abundance, readers are invited to explore how adversity can be a powerful catalyst for influence, and how, when wielded ethically, influence can uplift both individuals and communities.

Through the author's personal journey, we see influence redefined - not as a means to personal gain but as a tool for collective growth, built on integrity and genuine connection. As each principle unfolds - Reciprocity, Unity, Liking, Authority - Maria demonstrates that true influence is something to be earned, never demanded.

This chapter is more than just unlocking the secrets of influence; it's a practical guide, reminding us that in every hardship lies an opportunity to inspire, to lead, and to transform - ethically.

Vladimir Bushin

The Liking is King chapter reveals how the quality of relationships drives or blocks business.

Takeaways:

- You can think of relationships having 2 sides: disliking and liking, with respect in the middle.
- Disrespect creates an unsafe environment and prevents trust.
- Respect ensures fairness and, therefore, safety. When people feel safe, they experience trust.
- No respect means no trust. This means no business.
- When people like you, they'll also respect you. Build Liking and respect will be granted.
- Negativity is a sign of disliking. Neutralize it before any business.
- Connect on similarities and values early.
- Make people feel special and show them respect to activate Liking.
- If you are in a negative relationship, ask a trusted 3rd party to tell good stories about you.
- With credibility restored, negotiate respect back and connect on purposes.
- 7 Principles of Influence are bulletproof and tested by time. You can't lose applying them.

Christian Younggren

In The Experience Trap: When Too Much Sales Knowledge Becomes a Blindspot, Christian, a new recruit at a Midwest Chevrolet dealership, finds himself in an unexpected sales encounter. A disheveled customer, Butch, rolls onto the lot in a rusty old truck, and seasoned salespeople—including "The Hammer" Hank—immediately dismiss him based on his appearance and assume credit risk.

Christian's fresh perspective, free of these judgments, leads to a successful sale, highlighting a significant truth: experience can create cognitive blind spots. Drawing on behavioral psychology concepts like "fast and slow brain" thinking, the author explores how biases like Representativeness and Confirmation Bias influence sales behaviors and attitudes. These biases, along with Authority and Social Proof, often lead professionals to make hasty judgments and miss opportunities.

Through practical insights, The Experience Trap encourages salespeople to think critically and maintain open-mindedness to avoid the pitfalls of complacency.

Ellin Sidell

John Maxwell's "Law of the Lid" describes an invisible ceiling that constrains leaders and their teams from reaching their full potential. Whether leaders recognize this limitation or not, the result remains the same: diminished effectiveness and unrealized excellence.

Throughout this book, my co-authors and I reveal how "The Influence Advantage" serves as a master key, unlocking these barriers and releasing hidden potential within yourself, your team, and your organization. These evidence-based principles of influence can be learned and applied ethically, creating win-win outcomes for all involved. By mastering these principles, you'll develop the ability to navigate complex organizational dynamics and inspire lasting positive change.

Consider the opportunities and potential that may have already been lost behind locked doors of limitation. We invite you to explore how partnering with an experienced guide can help you use this key to unlock transformative results in your leadership journey and that of your team and organization.

Glossary

Authority Principle: A persuasion principle where people are more likely to comply with requests or follow guidance when it comes from perceived experts or credible figures. Displaying expertise through credentials, awards, or leadership roles enhances influence.

Cialdini Principles: A set of psychological principles identified by Robert Cialdini that explain how people can be ethically influenced. These include reciprocity, commitment and consistency, social proof, authority, liking, and scarcity.

Cognitive Bias: Systematic patterns of deviation from rational thinking that influence decisions and judgments. Common cognitive biases include confirmation bias and representativeness bias, which affect how people perceive information.

Commitment and Consistency Principle: The tendency for individuals to stick with decisions and commitments they have made, particularly when they are public or written. This principle can be used ethically by encouraging people to take small, initial steps toward a goal.

Confirmation Bias: The cognitive bias where individuals seek, interpret, and recall information that confirms their existing beliefs while ignoring contradictory evidence.

Conversion Path: A structured sequence of steps designed to guide potential customers through the decision-making process, from initial awareness to completing a purchase. Optimizing this path involves reducing friction and enhancing trust elements.

Emotional Reciprocity: The idea that emotional expressions, such as gratitude or kindness, often trigger a reciprocal response in others, leading to deeper relationships and mutual support.

Friction: Obstacles or barriers in a customer journey that hinder progress toward a goal, such as unclear messaging, lengthy forms, or complex navigation. Reducing friction can significantly improve conversion rates.

Influence: The capacity to affect others' behaviors, attitudes, or decisions through various techniques and principles, often grounded in psychological insights.

Liking Principle: The tendency for people to be more easily persuaded by those they find likable or relatable. Factors influencing this include physical attractiveness, similarity, and genuine praise.

Mentorship: A professional relationship where a more experienced individual provides guidance, support, and insights to a less experienced person to foster growth and skill development.

Micro-Commitments: Small, low-risk actions taken by a person that increase the likelihood of them making a larger commitment later. Often used in persuasion strategies to build gradual investment

Partnership: A collaborative relationship between two or more parties aimed at achieving mutual goals, often built on trust, shared resources, and aligned values.

Pre-framing: The practice of presenting information in a way that influences how it will be perceived before it is fully received. This technique is often used in sales and marketing to shape audience expectations.

Pre-suasion: A concept developed by Robert Cialdini where the context and timing of a message are carefully prepared to make the audience more receptive to the core message.

Priming: A psychological technique where exposure to certain stimuli influences subsequent behavior or attitudes without conscious awareness.

Reciprocity Principle: The psychological rule where individuals feel obligated to return a favor or positive action after receiving one. It is often used in marketing through free trials, gifts, or helpful content.

Representativeness Bias: A cognitive bias where people judge the likelihood of an event or individual based on how closely it resembles a stereotype rather than considering objective probabilities.

Scarcity Principle: The tendency for people to place a higher value on items or opportunities that are perceived as limited or rare, often motivating faster decision-making.

Social Proof: The psychological effect where people are influenced by the actions, choices, and approvals of others, particularly when they are uncertain. Common examples include testimonials, reviews, and influencer endorsements.

Sponsorship: A professional relationship where a senior figure actively uses their influence and resources to create career advancement opportunities for a less experienced individual.

Storytelling: The use of narratives to communicate messages in a compelling way. Storytelling helps build emotional connections and makes information more memorable.

Trust Signals: Indicators that convey credibility and reliability, such as certifications, positive reviews, awards, and professional endorsements, often used to reduce friction in decision-making.

Unity Principle: The persuasion principle where people are more easily influenced by those they perceive as sharing a common identity, values, or purpose with them.

Value Proposition: A clear statement that explains how a product or service solves a customer's problem, delivers benefits, and why it is better than competing alternatives.

Index

A

Abundance 59
adversity 9, 10
Adversity 59
Alchemy of Adversity 59
Amazon 27, 36
Anchoring 30
Apple iPad 51
Authority 60, 65, 83, 84, 93
Authority Principle 95

B

Be a Leader 46
behaviors 46, 98, 118
Be the Gift 44
Build Better Relationships 49
business 9, 25, 38, 67, 117
Business Administration 61
Business Enterprise 68
business growth 65
business owners 66
Business Profile 34
Businesswomen 58

C

Cautionary Tale 26
Challenge Assumptions 97
Cialdini, Dr. Robert 64
Cialdini Institute 69, 71
Clean Slate Philosophy 60
coaching 67
Coaching session 97
collaboration 15, 85, 97, 109
commitment 42, 57, 85
Commitment and Consistency 60
conversion path 25, 27, 115
Conversion Path 32, 119
corporate leadership 71, 110
Costco 110
Credibility 83
Customer Acquisition Costs (CAC) 38

D

digital marketing 20
diplomatic 61
diversity 41

E

ecommerce 26

Ecommerce 11

Ecommerce Marketing Expert 23

Ecommerce Success 25

education 57, 63, 64

Emotional Reciprocity 120

emotional struggle 60

emotional thinking 92

ethical influenc 9, 16

ethical influence 20

Ethical Influence 23, 65

Ethical Influence Coach 23

Ethical Leadership 70

F

Fairness 77

Familiarity 36

Fear of loss 28

feedback 44, 64

Finance Manager 87

financial services 66

Foreword 19

Fortune 500 113

G

Give More First 43

goals 21, 85

H

Home Page 35

I

inclusion 67

influence principles 21, 29

Integrated Marketing 23

Integrity 62

J

journey 71

K

knowledge 91

Knowledge 89

knowledge acquisition 104

L

Lack of trust 28

leadership development 57

Leadership Development 58

leads 95, 118

M

mentorship 103

Mentorship 102, 104

Microsoft 108

Mission 50

Moving Forward 53

N

Nestle 105

O

Online Success 25

P

Partnership 104

Prayer Warrior 49

Pre-suasion 29

R

Ratings and Reviews 33

Ripple Effect 69

S

Safety 76

sales 63

Sales Knowledge 117

Sales Manager 87

Serendipitous Encounter 43

Silent Killer 27

skills 41, 70

Social Proof 30, 95

T

The challenge 73

Trust 78

U

Unity 85

V

Volunteer 52

W

Website security 37

Winning Influence 103

Winning Strategies 104

Y

You are special 82

Index

www.ingramcontent.com/pod-product-compliance
Lightning Source LLC
Chambersburg PA
CBHW040436190426
43202CB00040B/2986